Legends of the
Lake Counties

by

Gerald Findler

Dalesman Books

1976

The Dalesman Publishing Company Ltd.,
Clapham (via Lancaster), North Yorkshire.

First Published 1967
Reprinted 1970, 1973, 1976
© Gerald Findler, 1967, 1976

ISBN: 0 85206 033 5

Printed by Galava Printing Co. Ltd.
Hallam Road, Nelson, Lancs.

Contents

The cover illustration is reproduced from a painting by Dennis Mallet. On page 42 the author tells of "a ghostly coach, drawn by four wild horses madly rushing along the road to Penrith ... There have been so many road accidents at one particular spot that the people residing nearby really believe that some uncanny force is at work that for one split second blinds the car drivers at night".

The decorations in the text were supplied by Edward Jeffrey, the late F. S. Sanderson, Sydney Buckley, Stanley Bond and readers of "Cumbria."

1.   Introduction

THE people who have been born in the Lake District or in the Border Country are naturally superstitious and more inclined to believe in fairies, giants, wicked spells, curses and enchantments than, perhaps, people from any other part of the country. Nature in itself is mysterious and magical, and the folk who live near enough to nature can believe almost anything. So, in the Lake District, we find each village and town has some sort of legend attached to it, some historical story that is passed down from generation to generation.

Mr. Whitfield M.P. speaking at Cockermouth in 1867, said:- "The various circumstances attending the growth of belief of spells and enchantments, of fairies and brownies, led to the conclusion that, in the Middle Ages, religion as then taught did not exercise any great influence on the Border." There is much to be discovered in the Lake District to confirm the supernatural belief of these mountain dwellers, of those who live near the lakes, or on the fells, or in the valleys. When one comes across some fairy pools or gruesome caves, how can one be anything but superstitious?

Helping to persuade these friendly folk that, in the early days, weird and unusual things happened is the fact that this glorious Lakeland brings out the poet in the poorest of scholars: one can well imagine that the bards and poets of the early centuries wove wonderful pictures in words to match their own flights of imagination. One can rightly say of Lakeland: "Which came first—the legend or the poem?" For whenever one comes across an old legend, there is usually a poem somewhere or other to tell the same story. While Wordsworth wrote of the beauties of the Lakes, other poets have struck further back into the past, and perhaps by some supernatural power, told in verse a thousand stories depicting this part of Britain, which has been steeped in history from the cave era.

Who are we to scorn fairy tales? Who are we to laugh at the four "Lucks" when one, the "Luck of Eden Hall", is carefully preserved in the Victoria and Albert Museum? Whatever we think or believe, these legends indeed help to make a place more interesting. A cave can be just a hole hewn out in the rock, or it can be the place where in years gone by there lived a giant or dragon. If we will allow our imagination to run riot when visiting such places, then it will certainly make our visit more exciting and memorable.

Dotted here and there throughout the Lake District we come across what are commonly known as Druid's Circles. Whether these circles were Druid Temples, or marked the places where the Druids were buried, or had anything to do with Druids at all, is a matter for much discussion. Of the Druids' religion any knowledge must be imperfect for it ceased to exist seventeen hundred years ago. Every locality had its deity and every stream its presiding god. The religious rites were all performed amid a grove of oaks in the deepest recesses of the woods and forests. The oak was a sacred tree and we are told that from its name in the Celtic language —Drui—their religion has been called Druidism and their priests Druids.

If an oak tree produced mistletoe, it was considered of special significance and a sign of Heaven's blessing. The priest would summon all his followers to a special ceremony, when two white heifers would be sacrificed beneath the oak tree branches, and the sacred plant would be cut down by the principal Druid. Feasting would follow. The Druids never

committed their doctrines to writing, though not ignorant of the art, but communicated all their rituals by means of verse, which the pupils learned by heart. Thus the secrecy and mystery of the Druids' ceremonies were preserved.

Their four principal festivals were held on 10th March, May Day, Midsummer's Eve and on the eve of the first day of November. Among the Druids was a specialised class of men known as Bards who devoted most of their time to poetry and the singing of warlike deeds of their heroes, mostly to the accompaniment of harp music. Perhaps many of our legends first appeared in some form of verse as sung by the Bards. The Lakeland, then as now, must have attracted the Bards, poets, versemakers or rhymesters, call them what you will. No living soul with poetry in his heart can fail to express himself among such wonderful surroundings as one sees in the Lake District.

One of the most re-peated legends in the Lake District and also in several parts of Scotland, concerns the large heaps of stones that one sees high up in most unusual places. How did such a pile of stones get there? The legends of these stones are similar in every respect. A giant or the  Devil was carrying stones in his apron, and for some reason or other the apron strings broke and the stones dropped in the pile as they are now seen. We find such place-names as "Apron Strings" or "Bratful" (which in this area means the same thing). The pikes on Carrock Fell and the stones scattered about the summit are attributed to the same Devil or giant. We find a heap of stones at Ullswater, which are said to have been drop-ped as Auld Sooty was striding from Nab to Burton Fell.

It is an undoubted fact that wolves once roamed about the Lake District. A cave known as "The Fairy Hole" at Hower-bank, near Milnthorpe, was explored in 1912. The cave has a very long subterranean course, and during the exploration a large quantity of bones of domestic animals were found, together with the remains of a few wolves. One part of the cave appears to have been a wolves' den in medieval times.

Many of the place-names in the Lake District were named after some "ulf" or wolf. We find Ullswater, Wulsty, Ulf's Ravine, Uldale and Ulpha. The legend of Wotobank concerns a wolf who devoured the Lady of Beckermet, and in the Inglewood Forest we find names like Wolfackes or Wolf Oaks. There are several Wolf Hows and Wolf Crags in Cumberland. There is a legend that the inhabitants of Talkin, near Brampton, were afraid to take the dead to be buried at Hayton Church because of the wolves at Geltsdale. The terrible massacres of Border warfare must have provided many a feed for the hungry wolves.

These legends have been collected from many sources. No doubt any keen member of an archaeological society could tear them to shreds and prove them to be fiddle-faddle but they were told, as they have been collected and written, to capture interest, and while historical research may prove them to be incorrect, they are still being told today—and believed by many.

It was Robert Anderson, the Cumberland Bard, born in Carlisle in 1770, who wrote about the strange superstitions and beliefs of the Cumbrians in his ballads in the Cumberland dialect: "The fault with the present age is not that it believes too much, but that it believes too little. Its Illuminati have ejected from their creeds not only the fables of the giants, fairies and necromancers, but the truths of revelation and the facts of sacred history. They wish to reform our politics, our philosophy, and our manners, and yet would take away that religion to which we are indebted for our public and domestic happiness.

"Were a missionary from this new school to visit those sequested parts of Cumberland, where the superstitions of our ancestors are preserved in all their purity, what stubborn tenets would he have to contend with? What shades of mental darkness would his philosophy have to penetrate? In almost every cottage would he see the Bible, and the histories of giants, fairies, witches and apparitions, occupying the same shelf, and equally sharing the belief and engaging the attention of their rustic readers.

"In the days of antiquity, the houses, woods and rivers of Greece and Rome were frequented by Lares, Fauns, Dryads and Naiads—all of them cheerful in their nature, and friendly to man. The Graces and Loves sported on their plains, and on their mountains the Muses strung their harps. But the Genii that haunt the romantic valleys, the hills, woods and rivers of Cumberland, are so mischievous and malevolent in their disposition, so terrific in their aspect, and hostile to the human race, that a person would be thought very regardless of his safety were he to entrust himself at any late hour of the night in the neighbourhood of their haunts."

Robert Anderson's summing up of the superstitious Cumbrian villagers over the past centuries may rightly account for the tragic nature of many of the legends. One can only say, in analysing most of the Lakeland Legends, that beneath each of them lies a lesson of brotherhood and good living, a lesson pointing out the punishment which is meted out to those who live by greed, to those who are cruel, to those who put gold before God. If the Lakelanders did keep the books on legendry, giants and fairies alongside the Family Bible, who knows that these humble folk did not see a closer connection between such volumes than the rest of the outside world ever realised?

2.

Kendal and South Westmorland

The Angel

A T Kendal we find an ancient inn called *The Angel* only a short distance from the original *Angel Inn* to which a legend was attached. It is reputed to have got its name from a miracle that happened there. On the occasion of the visit to Kendal of Prince Charlie and his army in 1745 some of the Highlanders, out to loot or destroy (an established custom in those days) are said to have raided this inn, which they found deserted except for a child who was playing on the floor of the hotel parlour. The Scots were about to seize the child when they were suddenly startled by the appearance of an angel who guarded their intended prey and drove them from the house.

There certainly seems to be a similarity between this legend and that of the "Angel of Mons" which the national Press recorded during the 1914—18 war, when Germans with fixed bayonets rushed over to the British trenches, only to stop suddenly as they saw a guardian angel standing near some wounded British "tommies." After the war ex-German soldiers vouched for this weird sight. Among the British solders were several from the Border Regiment, including a Kendal man.

Chapel of Ease, Kendal

A T one time, at number 20 Market Street, Kendal, was an old inn called *The Fourball Inn*. It was here that the local tradesmen would meet. They gave themselves the peculiar name of the "Fastossity Society" and the minutes of meetings are still preserved in a handsome oak box at Kendal Museum. It is here that you will find a very good model of St. George's Chapel of Ease. Tradition has it that the chapel stood over the vaults of a well-known wine merchant who, being a wit, and realising that such a peculiar combination could bring him more trade, had a sign painted and hung over the doorway of his vaults which read:

> *There's a Spirit above; and a Spirit below;*
> *A Spirit of Love, and a Spirit of Woe.*
> *The Spirit above is the Spirit Divine,*
> *And the Spirit below is the Spirit of Wine.*

The Devil's Bridge

F EW places can lay claim to more picturesque surroundings than the town of Kirkby Lonsdale. It has a most charming and romantic appearance, the river Lune, flowing from the fells down delightful slopes, flashing here and there over rocks, then onwards with a sweeping curve past the church and town above, through the golden glade and wood.

The Devil's Bridge is a remarkable structure, composed of three beautiful fluted arches. It gets its name because an old legend tells us that it was built by no other than His Satanic Majesty. If good can possibly come from evil, here indeed is a most splendid example. Every resident of Kirkby Lonsdale will tell you the legend of the Devil's Bridge.

A cow belonging to a poor woman had strayed across the river at some convenient wading place, and not having returned home at the usual milking hour the old woman went to seek her. But unfortunately the river had risen considerably, and the old woman was unable to cross, while her cow was isolated on the opposite bank. At this particular moment the Devil in human form appeared on the side of the river near the cow,

 and assuming the guile of the tempter shouted across the river that he would build a bridge across the Lune, on condition that the first living thing to cross the bridge should become his lawful prize. To this offer the woman gladly assented.

The Devil was cute, for he knew very well that her husband was on his way home from market, and hoped to make good booty. But the cunning woman was equal to the occasion. Seeing her husband approaching on the opposite hill, she called her dog and threw a stone across the bridge for the dog to get, much to the dismay of the Devil who was cheated of his prize. Below the bridge can be seen the Devil's Neck Collar—a rock with a large perforation, which is said to have been lost from his neck in his wild unearthly plunge from the bridge on finding his hellish scheme thwarted.

> *Now, crafty sir, the bargain was*
> *That you should have what first did pass*
> *Across the bridge—so now, alas,*
> *The dog's your right.*
> *The Cheater, cheated, struck with shame*
> *Squinted and grinned, then in a flame*
> *He vanished quite.*
>
> —From an old poem.

Kirkby Lonsdale Church

A magazine published in 1883 reported a legend connected with Fisherty Brow. Kirkby Lonsdale. "There is a curious kind of natural hollow scooped out where, ages ago, a church, parson and congregation were swallowed up by an earthquake. Ever since this terrible tragedy it is asserted that the church bells have been heard to ring every Sunday morning."

This is very similar to a legend concerning Kirksanton, and one wonders if the two legends were not one at some early date. the name Kirksanton being taken for Kirkby Lonsdale or vice versa. The legend of the Devil's Bridge can be attributed to no other place but Kirkby Lonsdale, so, in order to even matters, we'll credit Kirksanton with the original buried church!

Kentmere Hall and the Troutbeck Giant.

SOME four miles from Kendal is Kentmere, and here formerly was a lake which has now been drained. Kentmere Hall was famous because De Gylpin of wild boar fame once owned it. There is an old legend attached to Kentmere Hall. During the period of building it, ten men had been trying for several days to lift the heavy chimney beam into position over the kitchen, but had failed in their task.

It so happened that the Troutbeck giant, one known as Hugh Hird, was passing by as the men struggled with their heavy load. Smilingly he strode over to them, asked them what they were trying to do, waved them on one side, lifted the beam and placed it in its rightful position, which was six feet from the ground, where it still remains. This particular beam is 30 feet long, and 13 inches by 12 inches thick. It was said of Hugh Hird that for a pastime he would tear up trees by the roots.

Many records of the doings of this great Hugh have been recorded. Lord Dacre, who took a great liking to the hulking big fellow, sent him as a messenger to Bluff King Hal in London. It was a rough, tedious and certainly dangerous journey for any man to travel alone, but Hugh carried on with speed. The king received him graciously on his arrival, and asked what he would have for his dinner. He replied "The sunny side of a whether". The king's servants eventually found out exactly what a whether was, but knew not which side was the sunny side. So a whole sheep was ordered to be cooked. This enormous meal Hugh devoured, assisted by large flagons of wine. When he had finished his meal, Hugh stroked his waistcoat, and told king Hal that he had not eaten such a good meal since he left Troutbeck. The King replied that if all men

had such appetites there would soon be a famine in the land.

Other records give the Troutbeck giant's name as Hugh Gilpin. While some writers say Hugh lived in the time of Edward VI, the late Canon Rawnsley (an authority on the Lake District) assigns him to the reign of Henry IV. A further version has it that his nickname was the "Cork Lad of Kentmere" and he was the son of a Furness monk, his mother coming in disgrace to Troutbeck valley where Hugh was born. This version says the king was so taken up with the Cork Lad's skill in wrestling that he granted him the house and land nearby at Troutbeck for as long as he should live. After twenty-two years of enjoyment with his possessions he died of injury through pulling up trees by the roots. As he left no dependants the estate reverted to the Crown. It was later granted by Charles I to Huddleston Philipson of Calgarth.

The Witch of Tebay

MARY BAYNES, the witch of Tebay, died in 1811 at the age of ninety. She has been described as a repulsive looking woman, with a big pocket tied on her back. She had an evil reputation and both children and adults were afraid of her. Naturally enough, she was blamed for everything that went wrong—the witching of churns, geese, goslings. Even if a sheep, cow or horse died of some

disease the disaster was reputed to be the evil work of Mary
Baynes. So, because of her witchcraft, she became the terror
of her neighbours.

Ned Sisson, landlord of the *Cross Keys Inn*, had a dog that
killed old Mary's cat, so the owner decided to have her four-
legged companion decently interred in her garden and a farm
hand named Willan dug a grave for it. Old Mary handed Willan
an open book, and pointing out a passage asked him to read it.
But Willan, not thinking it was worth while to read anything
over a dead cat, held the animal up by one leg and said:

Ashes to ashes, dust to dust,
Here's a hole, and go thou must.

The old witch grew very angry, and warned Willan that he
would suffer for his levity. Soon afterwards he was ploughing a
field when the implement suddenly bounded up and the handle
struck him between the eyes, causing total blindness. Old
Mary was blamed for bewitching the plough. Mary Baynes
seems to have been endowed with some sense of prophecy.
Once when the scholars at Tebay School were out playing she
told them that fiery carriages would speed over Loupsfell
without the aid of horses. The London-Glasgow railway now
runs over the land to which she referred, at that time no more
than a large stinted pasture.

3. Around Morecambe Bay

The Luck of Levens

L EVENS HALL has attached to it one of the oldest deer
parks in England, and within its borders are some peculiarly
dark fallow deer. The local people believe that whenever a
white fawn is born in the herd the event foretells some change
of importance in the House of Levens. Four cases are recorded,
but there are said to be more: **1.** When Lord Templetown came
to Levens after the Crimean War. **2.** After General Upton's
death in 1883. **3.** On the day after Captain and Mrs. Bagot's
wedding in 1885. **4.** When Mrs. Bagot bore to Levens a male
heir in 1896.

Mr. Curwen in his monograph on Levens Hall, mentions the
following to illustrate the superstition which has gathered
round the white deer: "A white buck which had appeared in
the herd was ordered to be shot, but the keeper was so horrified
with the deed, which he thought to be 'waur ner robbin' a
church, that he actually went so far as to remonstrate with
Lord Templeton. Persuasion being of no use, he at last refused
point blank to do the deed himself, and another man had to
do it. In a few months great troubles came over the house,
In quick succession it changed hands twice; the stewards,
servants and gardeners all lost their places; and the keeper
held firmly to the belief that all was due to the shooting of this
white deer."

The Three Pillows

T HREE pillows or cushions appear on the coat of arms of
the Redmans, and according to the legend refer to a member
of the family in a fighting episode. The Redmans, originally

of Redmain, near Isel, and later of Levens Hall, were a well-known family in both districts.

One of the ancestors of the Redmans, or Redmaynes, had to fight in single combat with an adversary. He arrived so early at the place of combat that, while awaiting the arrival of his foe, he went to his tent and fell asleep. He was awakened suddenly by the flourish of trumpets which announced the alarm and presence of the enemy. Quickly rising from his bed he lifted his sword, ran out of his tent, madly rushed on his opponent and slew him without delay. The adventure was told and retold, and a perpetual reminder of the sleepy warrior was instituted when the three pillows were depicted on the coat of arms.

The Last Eagle

THE eagle was once a common bird in the Lake District and various reports show that eagles were still in existence there in 1777. The Eagles of Borrowdale are said to have been the last in the district. They settled themselves upon a rock at Seathwaite and crossed the ridge into Eskdale. The farmers, losing so many young lambs, organised themselves to get rid of the eagles once and for all.

The crest of the Stanley family bears an eagle and a child, and at Staveley the inn there is called the *Eagle and Child*. This is undoubtedly associated with the legend mentioned in Roby's *Traditions of Lancashire* concerning one Sir Thomas Lathom of Lathom Hall during the reign of Edward III. Sir Thomas had a daughter called Isabella who was most beautiful and refined, but he was disappointed that his wife had not presented him with a son and heir. He had an intrigue with a nearby yeoman's daughter, who eventually presented him with a son. He was

so delighted that he made every effort to introduce this illegitimate child into his own house in order that he could bring
him up as one worthy of high position.

He conspired with its mother to dress the baby in fine clothes,
which Sir Thomas provided, and to leave his offspring lying
on the grass in Lathom Park, on the path along which he and
his wife made a daily walk. The child was then discovered by
Lady Lathom, who believed her husband's suggestion that an
eagle had been carrying the child away and for some reason
or other had been disturbed and had dropped its prey on the
grassy parkland. It is understood that the daughter Isabella
later married Sir John Stanley and eventually came to live at
Lathom Hall. No doubt the yeoman's daughter in after years
would tell of her earlier experience.

Gilpin's Wild Boar

THE little river Gilpin has its source in Borwick Fold, and
after winding its silvery way for a few miles empties near
the estuary of the Kent. The stream has its renown, and is supposed traditionally to have received its name from Richard de
Gylpin. The De Gulespins, or Gylpins, took their name from a
place in Normandy and are said to have migrated to this part
of the country about the time of the Conquest.

Towards the end of the twelfth century a ferocious wild
boar roamed about the district, doing considerable damage
and causing many deaths, its den being in the depths of a dark
forest which stretched west and south of Whitebarrow to the
shores of Windermere and the mouth of the Kent and Leven.
The savage attacks of this wild boar became known far and
wide, and few dared pass the neighbourhood of Underbarrow
after nightfall.

A champion at length stepped forward in the person of
Richard de Gylpin, who tracked the infernal beast to its lair
in the intricate and dense gloom of the forest. A terrific fight
ensued in which, though severely wounded, de Gylpin came off
the victor, for the savage beast was slain. The picture of the
fight was for some time seen at Scaleby Castle which was built
by the Gylpins.

Cartmel Monks

CARTMEL is not only the name of the town and priory,
but also of the district which lies between the rivers Leven
and Winster. Cartmel dates back to the seventh century, when

the last King of Northumbria gave St. Cuthbert "the land called Cartmel with all the Britons in it."

According to local legend the monks arrived in Cartmel from foreign parts, and resolved to build their church on a hill above the valley. They spent many months clearing and preparing the site. One day when the monks were ready for laying the first foundation stones they heard a loud voice from Heaven commanding them to leave the site and build in a valley between two streams, one of which would be found flowing north and the other flowing south. In strict obedience they set out in various directions to find such a site, wandering about the Lake District for many months.

Returning to Cartmel to make plans for further search they crossed the valley, and in doing so forded two streams, One monk, more observant than the rest, noticed that they flowed in opposite directions. All agreed that this was the holy site, as one stream flowed north, while the other flowed south. Between these two streams they built a great priory. On the hill where they had heard the voice of God, they erected a chapel to St. Bernard. The chapel has long since disappeared. The hill, however, is still called Mount Bernard, and the remains of the great priory, with its beautiful wood carvings, stand today between two streams that flow in different directions.

Cartmel Priory

4. Central Lakeland

Calgarth Skulls

ONE of the most popular legends around Windermere concerns two skulls that could not be destroyed; although men had calcined them with lime, cast them into the lake and buried them on the mountains they would always reappear. Green in his Lakeland guide said that only one skull now remained and it was nearly mouldered away. Today all that is left is the story of the Calgarth skulls. They certainly have got more than their share of publicity for a poem "The Skulls of Calgarth" is to be found in *Folkes Speech of Cumberland* by Alexander Craig Gibson (1896). The skull legend was also written in novel form by Miss Strickland, titled *How will it End?*

Mrs. Brunskill in her notes on the Philipson family gave the story of the Calgarth skulls: "The legend runs that one Myles Philipson, a Justice of Peace, wished to add to his estate a small tenement owned by an old couple, Kraster and Dorothy Cook. The Cooks refused to sell, and in order to gain possession of this coveted property, Philipson invited them to a Christmas feast at his home. Afterwards he accused them of stealing a silver cup which he alleged to be missing. Somehow the cup was so discovered that the Cooks appeared as the culprits. They were tried and condemned to death. They were hanged at Appleby, but before her death Dorothy laid seven curses on Calgarth and said that while its walls stood they would haunt it day and night."

"Hark's to here, Myles Philipson, that teenie lump o' land is t'dearest grund a Philipson has ever bowte. For ye shall prosper niver maur, yersel, nor yan o't breed. And while Calgarth's strong woes shall stand, we'll haunt it day and neet."

It is said from that day forth the skulls have appeared at Calgarth, and returned there no matter what efforts the inhabitants made to be rid of them. Several people have gone to great pains to ascertain the true facts of the Calgarth skulls. The old house which was once the Cook's has disappeared, and a modern house is now built on the site. From records available, it appears that no Myles Philipson ever owned Calgarth. There was however a Myles Philipson during the middle of the 17th century who lived at Crook. He was a Justice of the Peace. Another member of the family, Christopher Philipson of Calgarth, died in 1634; he was also a Justice of the Peace. It is rather peculiar that, whereas up to 1634, the Philipsons acquired many lots of lands, after that date the family suffered and the estates became impoverished by fines, the price the family paid for its loyalty to the Stuarts.

To Calgarth Hall, in the midnight cold
Two headless skeletons crossed the fold
Undid the bars, unlatched the door,
And over the step passed down the floor,
Where the jolly round porter sat sleeping.
With a patter their feet on the pavement fall,
And traversed the stairs that window'd wall,
Where out of a niche, at the witch hour dark,
Each lifts a skull, all grinning and stark,
And fits it on with a creaking.
Then forth they go with a ghostly march
And bending low at the portal arch,
Through Calgarth's woods, o'er Rydal Braes
And over the pass by Dunmail Raise
The two the course are keeping.

—As described by a Dr. Alexander Gibson about 1880.

Crier of Claife

IT was at one time impossible to get over the Windermere ferry after dark, and if you were to arrive at the Nab too late you could call all night but the boatman would fail to answer your call. The reason was ably explained by the natives, who would tell you of the "Crier of Claife", the name of the ghost or spirit who has long haunted the district. Edmund Bogg wrote in *Lakeland and Ribblesdale:*

"During the 15th century, one stormy night, a party of travellers were making merry at the ferry house when a call for the boat was heard from the Nab. A quiet sober boatman obeyed the call, although the night was wild and fearful.

When he ought to have been returning the tavern guests stepped out on to the shore to see who he would bring. He returned alone, ghastly and dumb with horror. Next morning he was in a high fever, and in a few days he died. For weeks after there were shouts, yells and howling at the Nab whenever the night was stormy, and no boatman would attend to any call after dark.

"Things came to such a pass that a monk from Furness, who dwelt on one of the islands of the lake, was besought to exorcise the spirit of the Nab. On Christmas Day he assembled all the inhabitants of Chapel Island, and performed in their presence services that would forever confine the ghost to the quarry in the wood behind the ferry, now called 'the Crier of Claife'. Some say the priest conducted the people to the quarry and laid the ghost then and there. Laid though it be, nobody goes there at night!

"People still tell how the foxhounds, in eager chase, would come to full stop at that place, and how, within the last generation, a schoolmaster from Colthouse, who left home to pass the Crier, was never seen again. The Crier Quarry and Crier Woods are spots well known near to High Wray in a delightful wooded district, above the shores of Lake Windermere."

The Inscribed Rocks of Windermere

ON the eastern side of Windermere, at a point not far from *Low Wood Inn*, one comes across inscriptions engraved on the rocks. Much time and toil must have been spent on such engravings for the letters vary from six to twenty-four inches in height. On one large stone, roughly about ten feet square, is inscribed: '1833. Money. Liberty. Wealth."

Another immense surface of rock is covered with names: "Sun, Bulver, Dryden, Davy, Burns, Scott, Burdett, Garrick,

Kemble, Gray, Kean, Milton, Henry Brougham, James Watt, Professor Wilson, Dr. Jenner," and then in characters equally conspicuous is the phrase: "The Liberty of the Press."

On another rock one can read the unusual message: "National Debt £800,000,000. O Save My Country Heaven, George and William Pitt." And, all around other words

and names appear on these rocks. The man responsible placed his name on one stone, which reads, "John Longmire, Engraver."

It is said that Longmire spent about six years on this unique work. He was to be seen there chiselling away in all types of weather, and took pride and pleasure in what he was doing. That he was mentally deranged can be well understood, but at least he has left behind him a quaint monument which in a few hundred years from today will undoubtedly form some kind of legend, far removed from the actual truth.

Subberthwaite Moor

NEAR Coniston, on Subberthwaite Moor, two stone circles were discovered in 1842. They are known as the "Giants' Graves." Local tradition has it that there were giants in the district in the far off days. If these giants could roam about the Inglewood Forest near Penrith, as did Ewan Caesario, and in Troutbeck valley as did "Hugh, the Cork Lad," surely giants could also have existed in the Coniston district. So the natives firmly believe that these stone circles must mark the burial places of two giants, the last of them being shot here by an arrow from Blawith Knoll, a small hill some distance away.

Barbara and Girt Will

THERE is a long narrow mound near Yewdale Beck which is said to be Girt Will's grave. The mound is about four yards

long, and seems to be formed of solid rock, fitted close together, as if made by human hands. The legend dates back
some hundreds of years when the people living in these vales
were somewhat startled and afraid, having heard that one of
the Troutbeck Giants had arrived in the district and built
himself a hut, there to take up his abode in lonely Yewdale
valley.

Girt Will o't Tarns had arrived. Girt (meaning great) Will
was some nine feet six inches in height, but he soon overcame
the fear that was in most ordinary sized folk's hearts. He
showed his prowess at farm work, and was certainly useful
when he assisted his neighbours in repelling the roving bands
of Scots and Irish, who from time to time arrived in these
parts to pillage or destroy anything they could lay their hands
on.

On such occasions the defending force was under the
command of the Knight of Coniston, one Fleming, and Girt
was proud to follow such
a leader. Fleming was
advanced in age and, in
addition to his eight gallant sons, had one beautiful daughter, beloved by
all who knew her. This
Eva le Fleming had a
favourite maid called
Barbara who, like her
mistress, was endowed
with beauty far above
that of the average coun-
try girl. Naturally, with
such good looks she was
sought after by men from
far and near, but the only

man in whom she showed the slightest interest was the Knight's
falconer, a sturdy young man named Dick Hawksley.

One evening while out walking with her mistress, Barbara
related how, when she was returning from her parent's home
she was waylaid by Girt Will and, ignoring his advances
escaped him. Lady Eva was just expressing her indignation
when suddenly there was a crackling of trees, and from among
the broken timbers rushed Girt Will. He seized the screaming
Barbara and disappeared with her through the thick hazels.
Lady Eva, stunned by this sudden event, stood powerless and

then, recovering her senses, rushed back to the hall and gave the alarm, quickly explaining what had happened.

Dick Hawksley and a few of the men servants started off in immediate pursuit while half a dozen Flemings rushed to the stables and mounted their horses. Going through the wood at Yewdale they came in sight of the giant and his fair captive as he neared Cauldron Dub. The falconer called to Girt to stop but he continued with great strides until he reached the brow over the pool. Then realizing he was being overtaken by a strong force of men he uttered a shout of rage and disappointment and threw his screaming victim into the flooded beck and so continued his flight.

Hawksley rushed to the edge of the swirling water and plunged in. Those on the banks saw him grasp his beloved Barbara in his arms but the current was too strong for him and swept them down to the lake. The bodies, clasped together, were found several days later at the lakeside. Several of the men had left the ill-fated lovers to continue the chase of Girt Will who was finally caught and fought like a wild bull. But the swords of the Flemings proved too much for this simple giant and he was slain on the spot where his grave now stands. And so the Cauldron Dub is supposed to be the scene of ghostly apparitions—a wraith of a giant rushing aimlessly about the woods and, when the stream is in flood, to the screams of a drowning woman in her lover's arms two figures can be seen floating down the beck towards the lake.

On Styhead Pass

S PRINGFIELD TARN which feeds Sty Head Tarn at the summit of Styhead Pass was known in the thirteenth century as "Prentibïourntern" (or the tarn of "Prenti-bjorn"—meaning "barnded Bjorn"). Bjorn was an outlaw who for some foul crime or other was executed somewhere about this area and is said to haunt this wild mountain retreat. The place is the subject of a vivid description by Sir Hugh Walpole in *Rogue Herries*.

Wasdale Head

W ASTWATER and Wasdale are as grand a combination as can be found in the British Isles. It was an American who said to Nancy Price, "that it was the last place God made, and he had lost His touch," and Nancy herself said "Imagine a black mass of rock hollowed out by a great cheese scoop into the shape of a cradle; that was something like the effect the mountains and dales gave to me."

In the little churchyard at Wasdale Head one may find the graves of those who have died scaling the dangerous heights of the Gable and Scafell. In early days Wasdale Head was united with Eskdale for burials, and the coffins were carried on horseback across the moor.

An old legend of the district is known as the "Ghost of Burnmoor." A young dalesman had died and his coffined remains were being taken over the moor when suddenly the horse took fright at some invisible being, bolted and was lost. The shock of this happening so grieved his mother that she died, and at her funeral in the snow the horse carrying her coffin also ran off quite near to the scene of the first occurrence. A search being made, some men eventually found the first horse and completed the burial with reverence, but no trace of the second horse was ever found. It is now stated that in times of storm and mist, a galloping horse with a dark box-like shape on its back thunders past anyone who happens to be on Burnmoor.

Legend of Dunmail Raise

AS the stream of cars passes over the bleak road across Dunmail Raise, which lies between Keswick and Grasmere, little do the occupants of the vehicles give thought to the historic battlefield over which they are passing, and which holds a secret that no one yet has solved. For under the great pile of stones at the summit, lie the bones of Dunmail, last King of Cumberland.

According to the legend, Edmund, King of the Saxons, joined forces with Malcolm, King of Scotland in A.D. 945, and on the Dun Mail battlefield defeated the King of Cumberland. Edmund himself killed Dunmail on the spot where the heap of stones lies today. He ordered his men to take all prisoners to collect rocks and boulders and pile them on his prostrate victim to mark for ever the glorious victory. Edmund must have been exceedingly cruel for, besides killing King Dunmail, he also captured the King's two sons and had their eyes put out. The golden crown of the King was thrown into Grisedale Tarn on the Helvellyn range.

Early writers held different views and have gone to great lengths to prove that there was never a King Dunmail. The

heap of stones, they argue, was what was known in the early days as a "Dun." When two armies were about to fight a battle, each soldier of both sides placed a stone on the pile, and those who lived to see victory returned and removed a stone.

Other writers say the word "Raise" also means a heap of stones, and in one language the word "mail" is also given to a heap of stones. So we have Dun, Mail, and Raise, all meaning "a heap of stones." Most people of the district hold on to a belief in the legend of Dunmail. It would no doubt be sacrilege to remove the stones to find any evidence of an historic burial, but perhaps seeking for a golden crown in the Grisedale Tarn could be more exciting.

Clark's Loup

HOW do places get their names? Not all names are derived from the Vikings, the Welsh or the Celts—Clark's Loup or Leap is a much more recent name given to a rock which juts out on to Thirlmere. It is said to have been given that name after a man ended his life in a peculiar manner. This man Clark was of a jealous nature, especially as his pretty wife had so many admirers. He decided one day to commit suicide, and informed his lady why he intended taking such an action. First he suggested that he would go to a nearby hut and hang himself, but his wife said that was a very painful way to end one's life. Then he mentioned shooting himself, but she remarked that as he was such a poor shot at the best of times, he might not kill himself outright but would linger on and suffer needlessly.

He then spoke of drowning, and she told him that she had heard this was a most pleasant way of dying. So they went to the lake, and he proposed wading in, but she said the water would be too cold. Finally they both went to this rock that

juts out over Thirlmere and she advised him to run and leap from it into the deep water as far as he could so as not to hurt himself if he hit the rocks. So he took off his coat and shoes and leapt into the water. She stayed at "Clark's Loup" long enough to see that he was properly drowned, then went home quite satisfied in her own mind that she had done her duty by giving her husband the best advice possible.

Legend of Armboth House

FOR many years there was an innocent looking farmstead known as Armboth House on Armboth Fell, above Thirlmere, which over a century ago was said to be haunted. The legend is well known in the district. On All Halloween a wedding feast was being prepared for the daughter of the house, but in the midst of the preparations a man came rushing in to tell the family that the bride had been pushed violently into the lake and drowned.

According to Miss Martineau, in her *Guide to the Lakes* (1855), every year on this particular night lights are seen there and neighbours say that just as the bells start ringing, the ghostly figure of a large dog can be seen swimming across the lake. The plates and dishes clatter and the table is spread by unseen hands. That is the preparation for the ghostly wedding feast of a murdered bride who comes from her watery bed in the lake to keep her terrible nuptials.

Again in 1892, Mr. W. G. Collingwood in his book *The Lakeland Counties* mentions a nocturnal marriage and a murdered bride. Perhaps the best description of such weird happenings at Armboth House was given by Mr. W. T. Palmer in *The English Lakes* published in 1908. There he tells "that on a certain night all the fugitive spirits whose bodies were destroyed in unavenged crime assembled at Armboth House—bodies without heads, the skulls of Culgarth with no bodies, a phantom arm, and many weird shapes; the windows were alight with corpse candles, chains clank in corridors and there are eternal shriekings."

No records can be found as to who the unfortunate bride was, nor can any description of the murder be traced. No doubt the eerie Halloween visitors still play about the broad expanse of Armboth Fell.

The Hermit of Derwentwater

THE St. Herbert's Island of Derwentwater is well known for its beauty, but is perhaps little known for the legend that is attached to it. This pretty little paradise of four or five acres is well covered with woods and situated near the centre of the lake. It obtained its name from St. Herbert, a priest who chose the island for a sanctuary for his devotions. The remains of the hermitage are still visible, and near the hallowed ruins stands a small grotto of unhewn stone, called the New Hermitage, which was erected by Sir Wilfred Lawson in the closing years of the last century.

St. Herbert lived on a simple diet, mostly home-grown vegetables and fish caught from the lake. This was about the middle of the seventh century and he was very friendly with St. Cuthbert, the Bishop of Lindisfarne. They conversed a great deal, and so close a connection sprung up between them, that both these holy men expired on the same day, and in the same hour and minute, which according to Bede, was in the year 678 or 687.

There is little information recorded of St. Herbert, and but for his friendship with St. Cuthbert his name would not have been handed to posterity at all. He lived, prayed and meditated on this island. In the register of Bishop Appleby, in 1374, there is an indulgence of forty days to any inhabitants of Crossthwaite who should attend the Vicar to St. Herbert's Isle on the 13th April yearly (that being the anniversary of his death) there to celebrate the memory of St. Herbert. Wordsworth wrote the following lines of the Hermit of Derwentwater.

If thou, in the dear love of some one friend,
Hast been so happy that thou know'st what thoughts
Will sometimes, in the happiness of love,
Make the heart sink, then wilt thou reverence
This quiet spot; and, stronger, not unmoved,
Wilt thou behold this shapeless heap of stones,
The desolate ruins of St. Herbert's cell.
There stood his threshold; there was spread the roof
That sheltered him, a self-secluded man,
After long exercise in social cares,
And Offices humane, intent to adore
The Deity with undistracted mind,
And meditate on everlasting things
In utter solitude.

Legend of Lady's Leap

O NE of the ancient Lords of Derwentwater, who lived in a castle onLords Island, had an evil reputation for robbing and pilfering the neighbouring counties, and made the castle a storehouse for the large amount of booty he obtained. His sister who lived with him was a God-fearing woman, despised her brother for his evil way of living, and shuddered when he related his latest adventures and displayed to her the results of his plundering. So displeased was the lady that one day while the Lord Derwentwater and his men were pillaging near Kendal, she set fire to the section of the castle where all the treasures were deposited.

On returning, Lord Derwentwater discovered the cause of the fire, and the Lady, fearing his terrible vengeance, crossed over that part of the lake opposite the island, which in those days was fordable. In her desperation, and with determined effort, she climbed up the immense precipice and finally got to the summit by a track which still retains the name "Lady's Rake" or "Lady's Leap." The legend says that she made her way to London and lived in safety with relatives and friends.

Another version of the legend of Lady's Rake, however, describes the flight of the wife of the last Earl of Derwentwater, taking with her all the family's jewels to purchase the freedom of the Earl—without success. He was executed for treason and for his part in the rebellion of 1715. Some nights after the execution there was a great display of Aurora Borealis, and the people of the district afterwards called it "Lord Derwentwater's Lights."

St. Kentygern

THRELKELD, or Thelkret, is said to have derived its name from a Viking named Thorgell, who in the tenth century conquered the Cymbric people and settled in this beautiful valley. Centuries be-
fore, in the year 553, St. Kentygern reared a cross at this place and preached to its inhabitants. The mother of St. Kentygern was a daughter of the King of Cambria, and for her refusal to marry a neighbouring chief  was expelled from home to a life of drudgery in the field where she was held in ambush by the chieftain and indecently assaulted.

Her shame and sorrow being discovered, the punishment of death was pronounced and her execution was to be carried out by binding her to a chariot which was to be hurled from the top of Taprain Low. By some miracle she escaped her doom, so they took her to the sea shore, placed her in a coracle and without any oar or device to guide her, pushed the boat out to sea.

Yet again by some divine hand she escaped death, for in the early morning she was cast on the coast of the Firth of Forth. Here Thenew, for that was her name, gave birth to a boy, the illegitimate son of the chieftain. A hermit took pity on her and gave her food and shelter and tended to her in her plight. He named the child Cyentgen or Kentygern, meaning "Chief of the Lord." The boy grew up strong and healthy, and gained much knowledge from his foster-father, who was a learned man. Attaining manhood he travelled, first to Cathrures (Glasgow) and then on to Wales by way of Carleolum (Carlisle), but on learning that most of the people were pagans he turned west into the Lake District and baptized at Thanet Well. At Threlkeld he again halted, set up a cross and preached daily from sunrise to sunset. Here many people gathered to hear him, coming from the hills and fells from Derwent to the Greta.

Threlkeld Place Skulls

A similarity exists between the legend of the Threlkeld Skull and the legend of Calgarth Hall. At Threlkeld Place a skull was discovered by a new tenant in a small dark room that had been unused by his predecessor. It was promptly buried with reverence, but the wife of the tenant, going to the small room immediately after the burial to clean it out, was surprised and frightened when she saw the skull in the same niche in the wall where it was first discovered. The farmer, alarmed and no doubt afraid, carried it to St. Bees Head and cast it into the sea, only to find on his return home that the skull had travelled quicker than he had, for it was there in its usual niche.

Friends came to assist the farmer in his dilemma, and the menfolk made several attempts to dispose of the skull, but it was always back again in that small room. Finally it was bricked up in the wall, and the farmer and his wife quickly found another farm to work without any eerie companion.

Skiddaw Hermit

ONE of the most recent legends is woven around one George Smith of Banffshire, who in 1864 decided to get away frome very living person, and selected for his home a sort of a bird's nest perched on a ledge on Skiddaw Dodd. He used to get into his unusual abode by climbing, then dropping through a hole into a small cave. He had a boulder for a table, and his bed was made of leaves and hay. He walked about barefooted, and possessed neither hat nor coat. He would wash his shirt in a nearby beck and then put it on wet and let it dry on his body. Raw potatoes and anything else he could lay his hands on were his food. Later he ventured into Keswick and often got drunk on whiskey, so that the police were continually locking him up.

He was a very clever portrait painter, but gave all his paintings away free of charge, or perhaps for a whiskey or two. Some holiday makers, in a mischievous mood, spoiled his "nest"; and so he moved into Keswick, sleeping in any place that afforded a shelter. Some Keswickians said he had religious mania. Finally he died while on the way to his native Banffshire.

5.

Penrith and
Eastern Lakeland

Penrith Beacon Murder

THERE is a legend attached to a murder committed near
Penrith, which leaves local people puzzled to this day. It is
recorded that a local butcher, Thomas Parker, was murdered
on 18th November, 1766. One Thomas Nicholson was found
guilty of the crime and executed near the spot where the foul
deed was done, the date of the execution being 31st August
1767. Large letters cut out in the turf appeared before the
actual execution. The story should end there, but it doesn't,
for in the *History of Penrith* J. Walker says that the letters cut
upon the turf were T.P.M., which he interprets as "Thomas
Parker—Murdered."

It has been suggested that the letters on the turf were not
T.P.M. as originally thought, but were T.N., with the sign of
the gallows in between, the illustration of the gallows being
mistaken for the letter "P". Wordsworth commented on the
crime when he relates how as a boy he went riding towards
Penrith Beacon with a friend, from whom he got separated,
and while alone came across the sight of a gibbet where a
murderer was hanging in iron chains. He writes in his auto-
biography *The Prelude:*

The bones and iron case were gone,
But on the turf hard by, soon that fell deed was wrought
Some unknown man had carved the murderer's name.

Those letters on the turf still puzzle the Penrith people.

Eamont's Round Table

EAMONT, a quaint little village a mile from Penrith,
stands on the main road to the North, and is the centre of

much historical lore. It is here that one finds a circular platform or area known as King Arthur's Round Table. It is about three hundred feet in diameter, and is surrounded by a mound of pebbles twelve feet high. In this district, it was asserted, King Arthur's knights roamed in search of adventure. Historians tell us that the Round Table, like a huge cockpit, was formerly used for games, which took place in the middle on the raised platform, the spectators being seated on the surrounding banks.

It was near here that Sir Lancelot, the noblest knight in the country, slew the mighty Tarquin, and so liberated three score knights.

Nearby in the great forest of Inglewood, Paladin Rinaldo wandered in hopes of some encounter, someone to fight, someone to kill.

In his poem "Bridal of Triermain" Sir Walter Scott mentions the Round Table, as well as the Druid's Grove which is on the opposite side of the road:

> *He passed Red Penrith's Table Round*
> *For feats of chivalry renowned;*
> *Left Mayborough's mound and stones of power*
> *By Druids raised in magic hour,*
> *And traced the Eamont's winding way*
> *Till Ulfo's lake beneath him lay.*

Hart's Horn Tree

BROUGHAM CASTLE, near Penrith, is still a well-preserved ruin, standing on part of Roman "Brocavum," and was once the stronghold of the famous Cliffords. The surroundings are extremely picturesque, the castle rising from the south bank of the river Eamont just below its junction with the river Lowther.

It was during the time of Robert de Clifford that Edward Baliol, King of Scotland, stayed and enjoyed hunting in the Whinfell Forest. The legend says that Edward Baliol coursed a stag with a single hound for a great distance, dog and stag being so exhausted by the chase that both died. The stag leaping over the pales died on the far side, while the dog, attempting the same leap, fell dead before he could get over.

A memorial of this incident was considered desirable and the stag's horns were nailed to a nearby tree. The dog, Hercules by name, was given a decent burial. Over a period of time the horns became part of the tree, the bark growing over the root, and they remained there until the year 1648, when one of the branches was broken off.

The poem, "Hart's Horn Tree," describes the incident:

> *Here stood an oak, that long had borne, affixed*
> *To his huge trunk, or with more subtle art,*
> *Among its withering topmost branches mixed,*
> *The palmy antlers of a hunted Hart,*
> *Whom the dog, Hercules, pursued—his part*
> *Each desperately sustaining, till the last*
> *Both sank and died, the life-veins of the chased*
> *And chaser bursting here with one dire smart.*

Brougham Hall

A skull at Brougham Hall was said to give inhabitants many hours of fear. It certainly was most formidable and disagreeable; for unless it was kept in the Hall, the inmates were never allowed to rest by the reason of diabolical disturbances and unearthly noises throughout the night. Whatever was done with it, whether buried on land or in the sea, it had to be restored, in order that the ghosts of the former owners could rest in peace. To prevent any further contingencies this skull,

like that at Threlkeld, was bricked into the wall, and has given no trouble since.

Mardale—A Village of the Past

WHILE ancient legends abound through the length and breadth of Lakeland, what of the legends yet to be made, the legends of the future? One such may well be due concerning the village of Mardale. In 1936 one could visit the old world beauty spot, with its quaint tiny yew-shaded church, and the *Dun Bull Inn* with the great rhododendron bushes clustering around its outer walls. Today all is gone, for Mardale is beneath the lake which forms part of the Manchester Corporation Water Scheme.

This Mardale had its king in Hugh Holme, who fled north in 1209 after plotting against King John. He took refuge in a cave in the wildest part of Riggindale, which is known even to this day as Hugh's Cave. On the death of King John, Hugh still lingered in Mardale and founded the line of the "Kings of Mardale" which lasted over 700 years and ended with the death of Hugh Parker Home in 1885.

Up to the year ended 1729 it was necessary to carry the dead strapped to the back of horses, up the Corpse Road over Mardale Common and Swindale, for decent burial at Shap. I believe Hall Claine laid the scene of the *Shadow of a Crime* in Thirlmere, but wove his story around an actual incident that happened at Mardale. A prehistoric fort on Castle Crag at the head of Mardale remains above water level, to remind all. people of the future of a pretty little village of the past.

An amusing story was associated with Mardale church Having no one in the village who could play an organ, and having no organ to play, the vicar obtained an old gramophone and purchased some hymn records so that music could assist the church singing. The old verger would arrange the records and place one on the gramophone when the vicar announced the next hymn.

Two students from Oxford were amused at this unusual method and decided to play a joke. They went into Carlisle and purchased a new record, steamed off a label from one of the hymn records and pasted it over the label of their recent purchase. On the next Sunday when the vicar announced "Hymn number 135—Onward Christian Soldiers" the verger placed the record on the machine. Instead of the hymn tune expected, the congregation got a severe shock to hear the voice of Harry Lauder loudly singing "Wull yu stop yer tickling Jock?"

It is just one incident that may give birth to a new legend of the village that lies at the bottom of a lake.

Jimmie Lowther's Ghost

A T the Burne Bank end of Haweswater, Hugh Laithes Pike is crowned with a stone. This is said to be the last resting place of one Jimmie Lowther. Jimmie had the reputation of being a great sportsman, but unfortunately he was also a great drinker. One morning he mounted his horse for steeple-chasing while he was under the influence of drink, and before many miles had been covered he was thrown from his horse and met an untimely death by breaking his neck. It was said that, having died instantly, he could not make a death bed repentance and so became restless in his grave. He haunted the villagers in spite of every endeavour by the Lowther parson to "lay" the ghost.

So frightened did people become that it was finally decided to dig up his remains and remove them to some outlandish spot. So the corpse of Jimmie Lowther was removed and re-buried on the highest point of Naddle Forest, and a stone was placed there to mark his grave. After this the villagers were freed from Jimmie's ghostly visits, although people who have wandered near the summit of Hugh Laithes Pike at dusk have seen a weird figure wandering around the stone.

Dixon's Three Jumps

A NOTHER more recent legend is connected with "Dixon's Three Jumps." This is the name given by natives to Blea Water Crag, and it gained this unusual nickname in consequence of a remarkable fall from it by a man named Dixon in the year 1762.

Blea Water is an attractive mountain lake near Mardale. This particular crag from which Dixon fell is a good height, and on the day of his accident he was hunting for a fox, a sport which in many parts of the Lake District is done on foot. Dixon missed his hold and fell, striking the rocks many times as he was hurled hundreds of feet. He was terribly bruised, and almost scalped when he reached the ground, but fortunately no bones were broken.

On reaching terra firma, it is said that Dixon raised himself on his knees, and cried out in a loud voice to his companions: "Lads, t'fox is gane oot at t'hee end. Lig t'dogs on an a'al cum sean". He then fell back insensible. He lived for many years afterwards in Kentmere, where the inhabitants will still tell you about Dixon's three jumps.

The First Lord Lonsdale

OF Sir James Lowther, the first Lord Lonsdale, De Quincey said: "He was a true feudal chieftain, and in the approaches of his mansion, in the style of his equipage or whatever else was likely to meet the human eye, he delighted to express disdain to modern refinement by the haughty carelessness of his magnificence. The coach in which he used to visit Penrith was old and neglected: his horses fine and untrimmed, and such was the impression diffused about him by his gloomy temper and fits of oppression, that, according to the declaration of a Penrith contemporary of the old despot, the streets were silent as he traversed them, and an awe sat upon many faces."

If such a description be accurate, one can well understand that the people of Penrith and Lowther had many stories to tell of this eccentric Lord. One legend states that Sir James fell in love with a woman of no connection whom he casually met. He induced her to live with him and hired a fine residence in Hampshire for the purpose. It was doubtful whether the lady ever loved him, or was happy in the midst of such splendour. She was taken seriously ill and died, and so great was the distress of the earl that no one dared to mention the incident.

He refused to have the body of his late fair companion buried and when the servants complained about the unpleasantness of the decaying corpse he drove them from the house. At length, however, the body was placed in a tomb at Paddington and a detachment of the Cumberland Militia was sent to

London to guard the tomb for many weeks. This poor noble-
man mourned for his beloved until his dying day.

Superstition made his ghost more terrible than the living
man, for, according to the records of a Mr. Sullivan: "He was
with great difficulty buried, and whilst the clergyman was
praying over his remains, his ghost very nearly knocked the
reverend gentleman from the pulpit. When placed in his grave,
the power of creating alarm was not interred with his bones."

There were disturbances in the hall, noises in the stables at
Lowther Castle, and neither men nor animals could rest. At
length, after many an effort, a priest laid him under a large
rock called "Wallow Crag," and by so doing appears to have
laid his ghost forever.

Many years ago a native of Lowther, then residing in Carlisle, recalled that his grandfather often told him of a ghostly
coach, drawn by four wild horses, madly rushing from the
gates of the castle along the road to Penrith. This apparition
could only be seen on dark stormy nights. The coach was
supposed to have been carrying the spirit of the first Lord
Lonsdale. Whether this story was concocted by some superstitious old man as a means of scaring his young people I
know not; I am unable to find any printed records of such a
four-wheeled apparition.

On the other side of Penrith on the main road to Carlisle
there have been so many road accidents at one particular spot
that the people residing nearby really believe that some uncanny force is at work that for one split second blinds the car
drivers at night.

'TOWD YAK'
LOWTHER PARK

St. Cuthbert and Clifton

TWO miles from lowther Castle one comes to the pretty little village of Clifton. This place was the scene of the battle of Clifton Moor, when Prince Charles the Pretender fought the Duke of Cumberland. Histories tell us that both sides claimed a glorious victory.

The village of Clifton possesses a very ancient church, and also a massive peel tower of the fifteenth century. The church is dedicated to St. Cuthbert and, according to the local legend, is one of the spots where the monks rested during the long pilgrimage they undertook as they carried the body of the saint to its final resting place.

The strong peel tower with its stout walls, at one time a defence against many invaders, now remains a peaceful monument with the sun's rays throwing shadows on its sandstone walls, while the only signs of battle come from the crows as they fight for possession of some favourite nesting place.

Legend of Aira Force

THERE is on the western side of Ullswater a fine cataract, or as the Cumbrians call it, a force. It attracts many visitors and led Thomas De Quincey to write his "An Apparition at Airey Force." Wordsworth also penned a poem "Airey Force Valley." This same Airey Force, or Aira Force as it is now known, is said to be the scene of a romatic legend, which ended on a sad note.

Many centuries ago a castle was situated near the Force, and the Lord of the castle had a pretty daughter whose name was Emma. She was betrothed to a knight by the title of Sir Eglamore, who was a famous warrior then engaged in some Eastern war.

His long absence preyed on Emma's mind and affected her health. After many months of restless nights she fell into a coma and started sleep-walking along the pathway which is near the Force. It so happened that on this very night Sir

Eglamore was hastily returning to her side. Seeing her gliding along, he touched her, and she awoke with a start, only to slip on the damp rocks and fall into the rushing torrents beneath. The knight scrambled down the rocks to save her. She opened her eyes and recognised him before she died. The heartbroken Sir Eglamore never got over this sad loss, and built a cave near the Force where he spent the rest of his days as a hermit.

Aira Force Valley is described by the Cockermouth poet in his Guide to the Lakes (and later he celebrated it in blank verse) in which the following well-known lines appear:

> ... *the light ash that pendant from the brow*
> *Of yon dim cave, in seeming silence makes*
> *A soft eye-music of slow waving boughs*
> *Powerful almost as vocal harmony*
> *To stay the wanderer's steps and soothe his thoughts.*

Ghost of Greystoke Castle

IT must be an unusual castle that cannot boast of a ghost, and Greystoke Castle near Penrith is no exception. This castle was a stronghold of King Charles until it was successfully besieged by part of Cromwell's army during the encampment in the district. Greystoke Castle now boasts of a resident ghost. A disused room in the old tower is the supposed venue of its annual appearance.

Tradition has it that this is the ghost of a guest who once spent a Sunday hunting with Charles Howard, Duke of Norfolk. After an evening of merriment and feasting, he retired to his room at a late hour. Servants knocking on the door the following morning failed to awaken him, and finally an entrance was made to the room. His bed had been slept in, his clothes were lying about, but no trace was ever found of him, although an extensive search was made. Since then a ghost has appeared in the particular room annually, and it was said that anyone sleeping in the room was greatly disturbed during the night, even those people who were unaware of the tragedy.

There is also an old chapel in the grounds of Greystoke Castle, and another legend says that a monk was once bricked up in an underground passage leading from the chapel to the haunted bedroom previously mentioned. In past years, residents in the castle have heard knockings on the wall which is supposed to cover up the secret entrance to the passage.

Greenthwaite Hall

NEAR Greystoke Castle, just outside the boundary wall of the park, we find Greenthwaite Hall, which is considered to be a perfect example of its period. It was built in 1650 by Miles Halton and, although there is no trace of a previous building, it is recorded that the Haltons were residing at Greenthwaite as early as the time of Richard III. The Haltons hailed from Northumberland, and Richard Halton was the notable Bishop of Carlisle, also the custodian of Carlisle Castle, who is remembered for his battles with the Scots.

There is a legend attached to Greenthwaite that concerns a strong-minded woman, Dorothy Halton, who resided at the Hall. She would walk over the Greystoke Park and scatter a trail of green oats leading to her own estate. The Greystoke deer would follow the trail, and immediately they got over the boundary line they would be shot by cross-bow and used for food for the Greenthwaite servants.

This trickery was eventually discovered, and Dorothy Halton was summoned for poaching at the Cockermouth Assizes. When she entered the Court House, the prosecuting counsel exclaimed: "Here comes Madam Halton with her traps and gins."

Dorothy quickly retorted: "There sits Councillor Fletcher with his packs and pins." This reference was a "hit" at the commercial pursuits by which the Fletcher family had risen to eminence in Cumberland—a packman was a door-to-door salesman or hawker who sold pins, needles and thread to villagers.

Souter Fell Ghost Riders

IN 1774, a certain Daniel Strickland was out walking on Souter Fell on Midsummer's Day, and was startled by what he saw. There in front of him was a troop of horsemen, dressed in uniforms with which he was not acquainted, all mounted on fine look-

ing horses. He was evenmore surprised when the horsemen
rode up a slope far too steep for any horse to ascend. He
reported his unusual spectacle to the villagers nearby, and
it was discovered that similar incidents had been recorded in
1734 and 1745. The latter instance may have been a mirage,
a reflection of the Jacobite troops who were manoeuvering
some distance to the north.

It reminds me of a salesman who stayed at an hotel in Carlisle during the historic pageant week some years ago. Sleeping
rather late in the morning he looked out of the bedroom window to see Kinmont Willie and his horsemen galloping up the
street. He rubbed his eyes, believing he was dreaming, and then
seeing some passers-by in modern clothes, quickly realized
that it was no ghostly figures he had seen but some performers.

Perhaps the strangest thing of our modern age is the gradual
disappearance of ghosts in the Lake District. I can trace no
one who has seen the troopers on Souter Fell, and no person
who has heard of anybody else seeing them.

Scales Tarn

A small lake lies deeply embosomed in the recesses of that
huge mountain called Saddleback. It is said to be of very great
depth; indeed the natives will tell you that it is bottomless.
It is called Scales Tarn, and it is so completely hidden from the
sun that, according to tradition, sunbeams never reach it, but

Sir Walter Scott

the reflection of the stars may be seen on its surface at mid-day

As Saddleback is also known as Blencathra, it must have been Scales Tarn that inspired Sir Walter Scott, when he wrote that part of "The Bridal of Triermain" which reads:

> *King Arthur has ridden from merry Carlisle,*
> *When pentecost was o'er;*
> *He journ'd like errant-knight the while,*
> *And sweetly the summer sun did smile*
> *On mountain, moss and moor,*
> *Above his solitary track*
> *Rose huge Blencathra's ridgy back*
> *Amid whose yawning gulfs the sun*
> *Cast umber'd radiance red and dun.*
> *Though never sunbeam could discern*
> *The surface of that sable tarn,*
> *In whose black mirror you may spy*
> *The stars, while noontide lights the sky.*

Bowscale Tarn

A quaint legend is connected with Bowscale Tarn in the neighbourhood of Carrick Fell. It is in this miniature lake that two immortal trout for ever swim about in the quiet waters. Wordsworth must have been well acquainted with the legend for in his "Feast of Brougham Castle" he refers to the immortal trout:

> *Both the undying fish that swim*
> *In Bowscales Tarn did wait on him;*
> *The pair were servants of his eye*
> *In their immortality:*
> *They roved about in open sight,*
> *To and fro for his delight.*

King Arthur and the Giant

HIGH HESKET is a long straggling village, midway between Penrith and Carlisle. In its immediate vicinity there was at one time Tarn Wadlyn, a lake one hundred acres in extent but now filled up and converted into grazing land. On the crest of the hill on the north-east side of the lake there stood the ruins of an ancient fortress called Castle Hewen. It was at this castle, while King Arthur lived with his Queen Guenever in merry Carlisle, that there dwelt a man who was twice the size of common men. His wild, untamed nature made him the terror of all who passed that way, and this cruel baron took all that he desired. A fair maiden whom this baron had misused went to King Arthur and laid her sad grievance before him. He, in his chivalrous spirit, immediately set out to punish the baron for his infamy.

But this wild giant was in league with the powers of darkness, so that when King Arthur approached the magic ground upon which the castle stood, his courage vanished from him in some mysterious manner, and his sword arm hung helplessly by his side. The giant allowed the King to return to Carlisle in this sad condition, but promised him that he would be restored to full strength again if he returned the next New Year's Day and could answer the question "What is it a woman loves best?"

Arthur tried to obtain an answer from the gay ladies of his court, but neither they nor his knights could assist him. One day, however, while out riding alone over the fells, he was accosted by an ugly old hag in a scarlet cloak, who said she knew he had a question on his mind to which she alone could supply the answer. He promised anything she desired if she could give him the true reply. The old hag gave the information he required, and begged of him to marry her to one of his gallant knights. King Arthur promised to do his best for her, and rode to Castle Hewen. On seeing the baron, he told him he had the reply to the question he had been taxed with, and it was this: "Woman loveth her own will best."

The King returned to Carlisle and told his gay knights of his remarkable adventure, and how he had promised an ugly old woman that he would marry her to one of his knights. One loyal knight, Sir Gawaine, stepped forward and vowed that if the King so wished he was willing for such a marriage to take place. The ceremony was arranged and the marriage consummated. During the wedding night, however, the spell which had transformed the bride into an ugly and vile creature was broken and she appeared before her husband as a beautiful girl—the fairest of the fair.

Of Castle Hewen, where this giant lived, the annalists have only given slight notice. Leland, who wrote in the reign of Henry VIII, mentioned it as being in ruins at that time: "In the forest of Ynglewood, a VI miles fro Carluel, appere ruines of a castel cawled Castel Lewen."

In 1884, T. F. Bulmer wrote: "The foundations, which were visable a few years ago, show the castle to have been 233 feet by 147 feet, with walls in some places eight feet thick. Here dwelt, according to popular legend, Ewan Caesario, a man of

Giant's Grave, Penrith

gigantic stature, who rules over 'Rocky Cumberland' and who, if we are to believe another tradition, lies buried in Penrith Churchyard, a spot which posterity has named the Giant's Grave."

So we have to link up with Hewen, Ewan and Lewen. In St. Andrew's Churchyard at Penrith one may see the giant's grave. According to John Baron in his book *All about the English Lakes* it was opened some time between 1582 and 1590 by a Mr. Turner, when bones of a man of great stature were discovered. Another report states that the grave is that of Sir Ewan Caesarius, a great slayer of robbers and wild bears. He lived during the reign of a Saxon King named John, in the fifth century.

The grave is marked by two pillars, ten feet in height and fifteen feet apart, the gap being said to represent the height of the giant. Near the grave is another pillar known as the "Giant's Thumb." The official guide of Penrith says this stone is the remnant of a tenth century rose cross. We are told that Sit Walter Scott never failed to visit these remains of antiquity when passing through Penrith.

Quite near to Penrith, at Eamont, are some extraordinary openings known as the Giant's Caves, into which their grim occupiers are said to have drawn both men and beast and devoured them. Whether the Giant's Caves and the Giant's Grave have any connection is a problem unlikely to be solved. Probing antiquarians have decided the caves at Eamont were more likely to have been used as places of refuge; while the grave of Ewan was probably a Danish burial ground where several human beings found common sepulchre.

While I have written this legend in modern style from the details of the old legend, it is perhaps the forerunner of the thousands of children's fairy stories where the plot usually centres around some ugly old woman, or some wild beast, who becomes a beautiful princess, or a handsome prince, upon the breaking of an evil spell.

> *Noe gentle knighte or layde faire*
> *May pass that castle walle;*
> *But from that foule discourteous knighte*
> *Mishappe will them befalle.*

The Inglewood Squirrel

RHYMES or sayings give us some idea of the former extent of the forests and woods in the Lake Counties. We have the legend of the squirrel who could travel from Carlisle to Penrith, a matter of sixteen miles, without having to descend from the trees, this area being covered at one time by the well-known Inglewood Forest. A Lamplugh rhyme also states:

> *From Lamplugh fell to Morisbee,*
> *A Squirrel could hop from tree to tree.*

In his book *Lakeland and the Borders of Long Ago* W. T. McIntyre says: "At Lamplugh is, or was, preserved a massive table cut out of a single log of what is said to have been the last surviving tree from the once extensive forest of Lamplugh."

6.   The Eden Valley

Kirkoswald Church Tower

THE old township of Kirkoswald dates back to the year
1200, when a charter was granted by King John to hold a
weekly market on Thursday and a fair yearly on the feast of St.
Oswald, 5th August. Both of these are now discontinued, but
the charter is still proclaimed every five years. Kirkoswald
lies on the eastern bank of the river Eden, and is eight miles
north-east of Penrith. During the first quarter of the 18th
century, it was noted for a foundry, established for the casting
of church bells. The treble bell at Kirkoswald Church was
produced by this foundry, and bears the inscription "Aaron
Peever facit 1724."

The township, on account of its position, was liable to the
unwelcome visits of the marauding Scots, and from its records
we find it was burnt to the ground by Bruce in 1314. The
church, dedicated to the royal saint, Oswald, stands a short
distance from the town, behind a conical hill. Whoever
planned the building realised that the people who lived on the
other side of the hill would have difficulty in hearing the
ringing of the church bells, which were often used to warn
inhabitants of raiders. So, wise man that he was, he built the
church in the valley, and the tower containing the bells on
top of the hill.

A stream of pure water, issuing from a rock on the eastern
side of the church, flows beneath the building and may be seen
as it emerges from the western side by descending a flight of
steps. The Venerable Bede, in his history of the Church, tells
us that the waters of the stream where St. Oswald fell fighting
for his faith were celebrated during his time for restoring
health to man and beast, and that people also carried away
earth to avail themselves of its miraculous powers. This may

be the reason why churches dedicated to St. Oswald's honour
are usually erected near a spring or well.

The Renwick Bat

R ENWICK embraces the district lying between the rivulets
Croglin and Ravenbeck, north of the Penrith to Alston
road. The first recorded owners of the manor at Renwick were
the Staveleys, to whom it was granted by Henry I. Renwick
Church, dedicated to All Saints, was rebuilt in 1733 and again
in 1845 at a cost of £480.

A legend in the district states that when they were pulling
down the old Renwick church the people of the parish were
startled by a hideous monster, resembling a giant bat or
cockatrice, which flew around among the ruins. The workmen
who were doing the dismantling were filled with terror at
what they considered to be a vampire, so abandoning their
work they rushed to their homes, which they then barred up,
fearing immediate death if the bat attacked them.

One man, John Tallantire, was however more courageous
than the rest and, arming himself with a rowantree bough,
ventured forth to the partly demolished church. The huge
bat seeing human prey immediately attacked him, and only
after a strenuous fight did Tallantire succeed in destroying the
vicious monster. For this act his fame spread and his estate
was enfranchised to him and his heirs for ever. From this
incident all the villagers are still known as "Renwick Bats."

Long Meg and her Daughters

L ONG MEG and her Daughters is the name given to
what is known as a famous Druidical circle at Little Salkeld.
The largest stone is Long Meg, eighteen feet high, and her
family of some sixty-six stones vary in height from ten feet
upwards. It is said that if one continues counting them the
numbers differ every time.

One legend is to the effect that the smaller stones around
Long Meg were her lovers. Another legend says if a piece of
the stone were broken off Long Meg she would bleed, and yet
another legend holds that if anyone could count the stones
and get the same number twice, the enchantment would end.
I am afraid my effort proved unsuccessful, so Long Meg must
remain as she is.

A certain Colonel Lacy is reported to have attempted to
remove the circle by blasting, and during the time the work

was being put in hand there was a terrifying thunder storm, with lightning as had never happened before. The workmen who were there to do the blasting fled for their lives, and so to this day Long Meg and her Daughters—or lovers—still remain.

Wordsworth writes of this two thousand year old array of stones: "When I first saw this monument, as I came upon it by surprise, I might overrate its importance as an object; though it would not bear comparison with Stonehenge. I must say I have not seen any other relic of those dark ages which can pretend to rival it in singularity and dignity of appearance." He penned the following:

> *Speak Thou, whose massy strength and stature scorn*
> *The power of years pre-eminent, and placed*
> *Apart, to overlook the circle vast:*
> *Speak, Giant Mother! Tell it to the Morn*
> *While she dispels the cumbrous shades of night;*
> *Let the moon hear, emerging from a cloud;*
> *At whose behest arose on British ground*
> *That sisterhood, in hieroglyphic round*
> *Forthshadowing, some have deemed the infinite*
> *The inviolable God that tames the proud.*

Another legend of Long Meg and her Daughters tells us that they were a company of witches who chose this sacred spot to perform their infernal dances, and were, at the prayers of a saint, suddenly transformed into pillars of stone. Still another version invokes the aid of a famous magician, Michael Scot, who, it is said, endowed the stones with some magic power, so that no person could count them twice alike. The variation in the number of stones report-ed would appear to confirm this belief. Camden says there are 77 stones, Dr. Hood 72, Hutchinson, who was a great authority on Cumberland, said 67, and Jenkinson 68. My own counting came to 75.

Dick Whittington's Bells

MOST farmers in Lakeland keep a number of cats about the farmyard and barns to kill rats. They prove more successful at this game than dogs. One man famous for his exporting of cats was Dick Whittington, thrice Lord Mayor of London, and reputed to have been born at Great Salkeld. It is recorded that Dick was always enthralled with the sound of bells which, according to history, eventually marked the turning point in his life. But it is not generally known that during the height of his success he promised the people in his native village some bells for their church.

Great Salkeld is noted for its ancient tower and fine Norman doorway. The church, dedicated to St. Cuthbert, is one of several fortified places of worship one finds dotted along the border country. Its walls are six feet thick, and beneath the ground floor of the tower is a vault or dungeon which, when not in use as a prison, was a place of refuge for the villagers.

According to the legend, Whittington loved this old church and despatched four bells to Great Salkeld. When, however, they reached Kirkby Stephen some misunderstanding arose. Whittington had expected the Salkeld people to go and collect them, but they failed to do this, and so the bells remained at Kirkby Stephen and after a lapse of time were appropriated by the Vicar and Churchwardens at that place. The exact time is not known, but as Whittington died in 1434, at which period the present tower of Kirkby Stephen church was not built, it is quite feasible that the bells lay about for several years until a tower was built to house them. There were four bells in that tower, and around the barrel of one was the inscription: "Be it known to all men that see me, Thomas Stafford of Penrith made me. 1631."

The Luck of Burrell Green

AT Great Salkeld we also find the story of the Luck of Burrell Green. This luck is an ancient brass dish of ancient embossed work, circular in shape, sixteen and a quarter inches deep. At one time it appears to have borne two inscriptions, one in Old English letters around its central ornament, the other, not now legible, on the outer circle. Mr. R. M. Bailey, a London antiquary, tried to decipher the lettering many years ago, and was of the opinion that it was Latin and probably read, "Hail Mary, Mother of Jesus, Saviour of Man."

Like the other Lucks in Cumberland it has its legend. It is said that this Luck was given to a Great Salkeld family long ago by "Nob-i-th-hurst", or by a witch or soothsayer to whom a kindness was shown. On the day Burrell Green changed hands during the year 1896, the Luck fell down three times in succession from its usual position, a circumstance which up to that time had never occurred before, since it had always been kept in a secure place.

> If e'er this dish be sold or gi'en
> Farewell the Luck of Burrell Green.

The Luck of Eden Hall

THE most popular Luck is attributed to Eden Hall which has been made the theme for poems and articles. The origin of the Luck is that when a servant was going to fetch water one night from the Fairy Well, which is situated in front of the Hall, he surprised a number of fairies who were making merry in the moonlight. They were dancing round a goblet which stood on the lawn. The servant immediately seized the goblet, while the fairies gave the warning that should the goblet break or fall, the Luck would depart from Eden Hall.

The Luck is an ancient glass vessel widening by an easy curve. Its colour is green, with enamel of red, yellow and blue. One theory is that its origin was Saracenic, and that it was brought from Palestine by a member of the family during the Crusades. If care can preserve it, the Luck is safe in a leather case, adorned with vine leaves and having the sacred monogram "I.H.S." on top. It is said to have been stored in one of the strong rooms of the Bank of England during the last

war, but is at present in the Victoria and Albert Museum iu London. In 1934 the Eden Hall, built in 1821, was demolished.

Another legend of the Eden Hall Luck relates how a knight returning from the wars came accidently on the fairies disporting in the park by moonlight. In the confusion and flight which followed, the fairies left behind the cup, which the knight took possession of.

An old ballad tells a different story. A foot-page fleeing one night to Penrith to seek the leech to aid his mistress, the Lady Isabel, who lay in a deadly swoon, met a weird woman "wi glamour in her 'ee." The page-boy told her of his urgent message and he was advised that if the efforts of the leech should prove of no avail he must seek the fairies' well at moonlight. This he did, and the fairies gave him the Luck of Eden Hall filled with the spring water, together with a scroll upon which was written: "If that cuppe should break or falle, Farewell the Lucke of Edenhalle." The ballad ends as follows:

> Sir Ralph de Musgrave made a feast
>   For joy over his ladye;
> And the little footpage he stood by her chair,
>   And blithest of all was he.
> Sir Ralph de Musgrave built a church
>   In sweet Saint Cuthbert's praise
> That men might know when come the lucke
>   And think thereon alwayes.

Cross Fell

IF old traditions are to be believed, one of the most conspicuous landmarks in the North of England should be regarded as a memorial so far as the name gives. The legend is that the cross was planted by pious hands in early Christian days, on the summit of a range of those mountains which bound the eastern side of Cumberland, known by separate names, but collectively called Cross Fell.

This tradition is preferable to another which would lead people to believe that the cross was erected for the purpose of warding off the aerial demons which were thought to possess these desolate regions. There is no doubt that such a belief was strongly held, for the name Fiend's Fell is a clear indication. Some say that the bodies of the Christians who died in the heathen districts were carried across the fell ('Cross t' Fell') to be buried in consecrated ground.

Bewley Castle Legend

THE neighbourhood of Bewley Castle, Bolton, has been the scene of many daring skirmishes and attempted raids. A legend attached to the castle takes us back to a wild and wintry evening at the end of October, 1598. The family had gone to some friends at King's Meaburn, and the only occupant of Bewley was an old god-fearing house-keeper named Margaret Dawe. "Margaret" as she was called, had put the bolts in the massive oak door and returned to the kitchen where, sitting near the huge log fire, she busied herself making rush lights, plaiting the rush piths and then dipping them in the melted tallowfat.

She had been working for an hour or so when a knock came at the door. Opening it she perceived a tall though decrepit woman standing on the threshold who, in a deep harsh voice, begged food and rest. Margaret beckoned the woman in, fed

her, and pressed her to drink some home-brewed ale. The stranger, having satisfied her hunger and thirst, dropped off to sleep. It was then that the old house-keeper noticed that the stranger was wearing man's top boots, adorned with large steel spurs. Looking closer at the face of the sleeping figure, Margaret quickly realised that it was no woman at all, but a man in disguise, and certainly up to no good.

So she picked up a ladle, dipped it into the hot tallowfat.
and poured the liquid down the open mouth of the sleeper,
A loud yell followed as the figure rolled on to the floor in
great agony. Hearing a low whistle outside, Margaret rushed
up to the pele tower and rang the bell of alarm furiously.

Soon there was firing of pistol shots outside the castle, and
then came the voice of Sir Richard Musgrave, her master,
telling her to open the door. Sir Richard and his son, hearing
the castle bell, had quickly arrived on the scene and had
driven the raiders away. The prostrate body of the disguised
man, now dead, turned out to be none other than Belted Will
Scott, one of the most notorious freebooters on the Border.
A. Whitehead has related in *Legends of Westmorland:* "Then
they trailed the body of the man-woman far into the forest
and buried him snugly under some trees. Though unshrouded
or shriven he got extreme unction. At least summet like it, wi
het cannel grease".

Peg Sleddall

A N apparition is associated with the ancient family of
Machell of Crackenthorpe Hall near Appleby. It was
Lancelot Machell who tore up Cromwell's new charter for
Appleby in open court. Lancelot married a Miss Elizabeth
Sleddall of Penrith. She was executrix of her husband's will,
and for some alleged injury to her husband's estate, it is said,
she swore vengeance and after her death she paid the Machells
ghostly visitations whenever the head of the family was about to
die. Appleby people say she was buried beneath a large stone,
known as Peg's Stone, near Crackenthorpe Hall.

It was told me during my brief stay at Appleby as a con-
valescent soldier during the first World War that Peg had
been seen driving at great speed along the Appleby roads,
with amber lights in the carriage, the coach disappearing
suddenly when it approached Machell Wood, at a place now
named Peg Sleddall's Trough.

Whether as the years roll by the legend grows more elaborate
I know not. It is said that when the weather is stormy Peg
appears in an angry mood, and she appears in a merry mood
when it is fine. In the same district is an old tree called Sleddall's
Oak, and Peg is said to sit here and weep when any member
of the Machell family suffers misfortune. I could find no
Machells during my stay, but in those far off army days the

wounded "Tommies" who were in Appleby often came in at night with gruesome stories of having seen Meg.

The Ghost of Crosby Hall

CROSBY HALL, Crosby Ravensworth, was pulled down several years ago. Whether its demolition was due to almost nightly visits of what the Lakelanders call a "dobbie" or ghost, or whether it was in poor state of repair, I know not.

The legend says that the "dobbie" took various shapes. At some periods in the shape of a big white bull it would lick the window panes of the hall, or at other times it would appear as a huge bat. On some nights the mantle tower would shake, or the bell would be tolled by an unseen force. Pictures would swing on the walls and plates would rattle on the kitchen shelves. It is recorded that when the tower was dismantled this supernatural being ceased its visits, but not until it had disclosed to the old keeper of the hall the secret hiding place of some valuable treasures. The old man, the same night, was informed of the time and nature of his death.

> *And thus it carried on for years,*
> *To think on't makes yan whidder,*
> *Till t'auld man cock'd his head—an' then*
> *They breathe went off to gidder.*

Another version of the legend suggests that the old man himself was instrumental in killing his lawful heir and was continually haunted as a revenge for his crime. The haunted hall caused terror and excitement among the people of Crosby Ravensworth, and they were not sorry when the entire building was demolished.

The Church at Crosby Garrett

CROSBY GARRETT is three miles from Kirkby Stephen, and stands in the valley at the foot of Crosby Fell. The church there occupies a high position just north of the village. On this hill, some early missionary raised a cross as the symbol of christianity, and the village rose in the valley; hence the name Crosby, the village by the cross.

The church is a very interesting structure and a conspicuous object for miles around. Legend says that the villagers started to build the church in the valley, and material for its construction was carried there by daytime. But during the stillness of the night some unseen power of great strength removed all the huge timbers and stones and placed them at the top of the hill. In great fear and after long discussion, the villagers decided to build their church on the site where the materials were lying, and there to this day the church stands, the church that was intended to be built in the valley.

The Devil's Mustard Mill

A T Stenkrith Bridge, near Kirkby Stephen, a subterranean stream causes a rumbling sound which gives the effect of some uncanny machinery at work, deep in the bowels of the earth. It is easily understood, then, that the simple and superstitious country folk should associate such weird underground noises with the Prince of Darkness. Others thought that some witch had been thrown in the stream and made her way into the bowels of the earth to continue her magic.

Uther Pendragon

A T one time all giants were outcasts, believed to be both sinister and cruel. But while the Lakeland giants were to be feared, only in isolated cases is it recorded that these hulking fellows committed any acts of violence. One Hugh Hird, described in another legend, was by all accounts a likeable kind of chap, and his wrestling feats and demonstrations of pulling up trees by the roots earned him a country-wide reputation.

Perhaps one of the most ancient of the north-western giants was Uther Pendragon, father of King Arthur. No kindly giant was this Uther. He was a cannibalistic tyrant. He founded his kingdom in Mallerstang, which his son King Arthur extended up into Scotland in the north, and over to Yorkshire in the east. Of Uther Pendragon it is recorded down the ages that he occupied his time trying to divert the river Eden so that it would form a moat to his castle. As a wise poet wrote:

> *Let Uther Pendragon do what he can*
> *Eden shall run as Eden ran.*

It is stated that travellers going over Shap Fells on wintry nights have seen in the distance a ghostly figure of a giant, mounted on a mighty horse galloping at a tremendous speed. Perhaps Uther Pendragon can find no peace, as a penance for his mode of living on this earth when he gave no peace to any man.

The legend of Uther Pendragon refers to Pendragon Castle, now only a scanty ruin in the wilds of the Mallerstang Gorge of the upper Eden. The castle was his abode. It was Uther who led the Cymric, and fought bravely against the Saxons both in the west and north country. He died by drinking water from a poisoned well, and young Arthur, the peerless knight, succeeded to the royal dignity.

The Uther Pendragon castle passed on to the families of Vipont and Clifford. The Scots destroyed what they could of it by fire in 1341 and Roger de Clifford restored it between the years 1360-70. Two hundred years after their first effort the Scots again set it on fire, and it lay in ruins until Lady Anne Clifford rebuilt it. After her death it was dismantled in 1685 by the Earl of Thanet. In 1773 the greater part of it fell down and decay continued down the years until the remains were taken over and preserved. The local legend says that deep beneath the foundations of the castle a great treasure has remained hidden ever since the days of Merlin, the great Arthurian bard.

Lady Anne Clifford

The Headless Horsewoman of Stainmoor

A BOVE the Eden Valley is a wild stretch of fell land around the Pass of Stainmoor. It was here, according to tradition, that during the period when the Norsemen invaded England the Danish King Eric was killed. It is natural, then, that such a wild and desolate place should have its legends. A moor where battles were fought, and where the wolf, wild boar and red deer roamed, a place where the Normans built strongholds, and the Romans before them built a road, is a veritable trove for folk-lore.

It was a "not-too-well-read" lorry driver who told me that during the winter of 1937 he was snow-bound with his lorry and had to sit in the cabin all night. Taking a walk in the early hours of the morning to keep himself warm, he was scared stiff when he saw a headless woman riding on a large horse at great speed across the moor. Turning up all reference books which might be connected with Stainmoor in the hope of finding some explanation, I came across this legend, recorded by Edmund Bogg in his book *A Thousand Miles of Wandering along the Roman Way*.

"A Saxon chieftain dwelt in a rude fortress on the edge of Stainmoor, acknowledging no king as his master, and between him and Fitz-Barnard the Norman, whose stronghold was by the rushing Tees, was a bitter hatred, perhaps from the natural antipathy between the two races or possibly over the right to chase on the moor which both claimed as their own.

"Be that as it may, the two parties had more than once come to blows whilst hunting, and in one encounter several retainers and the daughter of Fitz-Barnard, a beautiful girl of some twenty summers, were taken prisoners. The object of the chieftain was to make her his wife, and she was treated with all the courtesy and kindness possible in that rude age.

"All his attempts to win her love were, however, fruitless, and after remaining a prisoner for some time she was rescued by stratagem, and was being borne triumphantly across the moor when the Saxon appeared on the scene with a number of retainers and charged madly into the group of rescuers who were unable to withstand the onslaught. The chieftain, furious at the thought of losing his fair captive, with one savage stroke severed the head of the young Norman from her body. Hence is the headless horsewoman seen galloping at midnight over the moor."

My lorry-driver friend may have heard a version of this legend, which is not so well known; or perhaps he did see the ghostly figure riding headless across Stainmoor in 1937.

Mortham's Tower

BEYOND Stainmoor are Greta Bridge and Rokeby Woods. Near Mortham's tomb is an old Border Pele tower, and connected with it is a grim legend. Hundreds of years ago a certain Lord of Rokeby, in a fit of frenzy caused by incessant jealousy, murdered his wife in the glen below the tower, and the bloodstains which cannot be effaced are still to be seen on the steps. It is said they were caused by the blood dripping from his dagger as he mounted the stairs after committing the fearful crime.

For years afterwards the ghostly spirit of the murdered woman haunted Mortham's Tower and the vale of Greta. This spectral visitor appeared so often and scared so many people that the services of a parson were requested. On a specified day he attended the tower with the Bible in his hand, read the spirit down, then confined her under the bridge. During the great floods of 1771, the bridge was swept away and with it the spirit, for it has not been heard of since:

> *The 'lated peasant shunned the dell,*
> *For superstitions wont to tell*
> *Of many a ghostly sound and sight*
> *Scaring its path at dead of night.*

7.

Along the Cumberland Coast

Kirksanton

A LEGEND associated with West Cumberland is that of Kirksanton, near Millom. There is a basin or hollow in the surface of the ground, assigned as a place where once stood a church that was swallowed up when the earth opened and then closed over it bodily. It used to be believed that on Sunday mornings the bells of the church could be heard ringing far down in the earth by any who would perform the simple act of putting an ear to the ground.

The Luck of Muncaster

THE Luck of Muncaster is said to be a gift of Henry the Sixth, who stayed for a brief spell with the Penningtons, the owners of Muncaster. It was about 1464, and the King had lost a number of powerful followers after the Battle of Hexham. He turned to the owner of Muncaster who vowed his staunch support and kept the King in safety. The room in which the monarch slept is still preserved with great care, and the carved oak bedstead on which he rested bears his initials and a crown.

To mark his appreciation, Henry presented to Sir John Pennington a glass cup or basin, ornamented with gold and white enamel. It was given with the assurance that "the family shall prosper so long as they preserve this cup unbroken." The Luck of Muncaster is the subject of a poem, illustrating the evil designs of a kinsman who tried to destroy the cup and the Pennington fortune alike.

In the castle are two oil paintings, one representing the King giving the cup to Sir John Pennington, and the other showing the king holding the Luck. On an old stone in Muncaster church is the inscription: "Holie Kynge Harrye gave Sir John a brauve workyd glass cuppe . . . whykkys the famylie shold keep it unbrecken thei shold gretelye thrif."

Calder Abbey

WHILE the monastic houses at Carlisle, Holme Cultram, St. Bees and Lanercost are still in use, the only monastic ruin to be seen in Cumberland is that of Calder Abbey. It is a lovely ruin standing in the delightful valley of the Calder, only a few miles in distance yet eight centuries away from man's latest creation, the atomic plant at Calder Hall. Calder Abbey in its situation reminds one of Furness Abbey. The resemblance is understandable, because the first founders of the former were the Savigian monks from the latter.

According to records "Gerald with twelve companions was dispatched to found the Abbey of Calder, but having reached their destination and being settled there for four years, one, David of Scotland, making an inroad into Cumberland, plundered the newly founded Abbey, and Gerald with his companions fled, terrified and made their way back to the mother monastery at Furness. This happened about the third year of King Stephen. The Abbot at Furness refused to see Gerald and his men, reproaching them with cowardice for abandoning the monastery, and alleging it was the love of that ease and plenty which they expected in Furness, rather than the devastations of the Scottish army, that forced them from Calder".

Some writers say that the Abbot of Furness insisted that Gerald should divest himself of his authority, and absolved the monks from their obedience to him as a condition of their receiving any relief or again being admitted into their old monastery. This Gerald and his companions refused to accept and turning their faces from Furness, they, with the remains of their broken fortune, which consisted of little more than some clothes and a few books, one cart and eight oxen, took Providence for their guide and went in search of better hospitality, eventually founding the Byland Abbey in Yorkshire. In 1148 another colony of Cistercian monks was founded at Calder under the rule of Hardred, who built the Abbey, a beautiful structure, until it was finally destroyed by Robert the Bruce. The monks at Calder used neither fur nor linen, and never ate flesh except in times of dangerous sickness.

> *Alas for man's frail work! What mighty wrecks*
> *Of grandeur past are here! Say, ruined wall—*
> *Ye ivy-clad and mouldering arches,—say,*
> *Where are your ancient inmates? They are gone!*
> *In lone cells, where erst the voice of prayer*
> *Was hourly breathed, the night wind whistles chill;*
> *And now, where once the solemn hymn and chant*
> *Were echoed through the dim and stately aisles,*
> *The wild bird builds her nest and warbling there*
> *Trills her sweet lay, unmindful of the Past.*
> —Anon.

Ehenside Tarn

EHENSIDE or Gibb Tarn, one of a group of tarns which exist or formerly existed in a strip of land south of Nethertown, lies between the river Ehen and the sea. W. T. McIntyre records in his book *Lakeland and the Borders of Long Ago* the draining of the five-acre Ehenside Tarn in 1869 by a John Quayle.

This task produced definite evidence that the bottom of the tarn had been an ancient human settlement. The remains discovered consisted of firehearths, pottery, stone implements, wooden clubs, and a stone axe still fixed in its wooden handle—this last named now being an exhibit at the British Museum.

The Horn of Egremont

QUITE near the atomic energy plant at Calder Hall lies the small market town of Egremont. The granting of its charter dates back to 1267, and it is overlooked by the ruins of its great castle, built about 1170. The legend known as the "Boy of Egremont" is traditionally concerned with young William de Romilli, nephew of David I of Scotland, and son of Lady Alice de Romilli of Keswick. William, it is recorded, was sole heir to wide lands, and might have been King of Scotland; so many fair hopes perished with him and there was endless sorrow when he was accidentally drowned. The story of the "Horn of Egremont" which could only be sounded by the rightful Lord of Egremont Castle was retold by Wordsworth.

Another version said "a son of Lady Alice de Romilli was supposed to be drowned when returning from a hunt. A de Romilly was drowned in the Wharfe at Strid, but it was not 'the boy' as he was alive as late as the year 1160." A further legend concerning Egremont, or the Mount of Sorrow, is

—Egremont Castle

connected with two brothers named "de Lacey." At the castle gate was hung the famous horn which no one could blow except the rightful owners of the estate.

The two brothers, Sir Eustace and Hubert started for the Holy Wars, and just before leaving the elder blew the horn, saying to his brother, "If I fall in Palestine, do thou return and blow this horn and take possession, that Egremont may not be without a de Lacy for its Lord." While in Palestine Hubert, anxious to obtain possession of the Egremont estates, hired some assassins to drown his elder brother and paid them well for their evil work.

Some time afterwards Hubert returned to Egremont and took possession of the castle, but dared not blow the horn. Many months elapsed. Then one day, while a great banquet was being held prior to a hunt, the horn sounded loud and clear. Immediately Hubert knew that his brother was still alive and had arrived at the castle. He quickly escaped and wandered about the Lake District for many years, until finally he returned and begged forgiveness, which was readily given on condition that he entered a convent. Egremont castle was besieged by Robert Bruce and by Lord James Douglas, but it survived until all but the court-house was destroyed in 1578.

Wotobank

A few legends of the Lake District come down to us of the days when wolves roamed about the wild stretches of fell and mountain. One concerns a lady belonging to the Lucy family who were the great territorial lords of West Cumberland. One evening this lady was walking near Egremont Castle when she was attacked and devoured by a wolf. The place was afterwards marked by a stone cairn, and known as Woful Bank.

The legend is that Edgar, a lord of Beckermet, and his Lady Edwina with their servants were out hunting wolf in the forests near Egremont Castle. During the chase the lord missed his lady. After a long and painful search the party found her lying on the hill slain by a wolf, with the ravenous beast still in the act of tearing the body to pieces and devouring it. In his sad grief and distress, the lord uttered the words, "Woe to this bank," a phrase since altered and applied to the place as "Wotobank."

In the middle of the last century it was recorded that a ghostly wolf haunted the vicinity of Wotobank. Several sheep were found torn to pieces and the wolf was blamed by the people of the district until one evening at dusk a farmer saw a ghostly figure attacking a sheep, and immediately shot it. On examining his victim the farmer discovered it was a large dog. After that episode the ghost wolf disappeared. Another wolf legend of a similar character is attached to a well called Lady's Dub, at Ulpha.

Legend of St. Bega

THE pretty little resort of St. Bees, with its grey roofed houses, lying peacefully in the valley near the rose pink cliffs

—St. Bees

of St. Bees Head, is linked up with the beautiful legend of St. Bega, from whom it is said to have derived its name.

Many ships have been wrecked at St. Bees Head, and the lighthouse has prevented many more losses at sea. The legend concerns a ship-wreck off St. Bees Head when St. Bega, an Irish nun, and a number of Sisters, were washed ashore about the middle of the seventh century. Most of them survived, and as they lay exhausted on the shore, St. Bega, in her distress went to Egremont Castle to beg relief and accommodation for her unfortunate companions and herself. Lady Egremont willingly agreed and gave them food and shelter. Her ladyship struck up a close friendship with St. Bega, and promised to do the utmost in her power to persuade her husband to provide the land and materials to build a sanctuary where the nuns and others could lead a religious life together.

On making her unusual request to her husband, Lady Egremont was answered not too satisfactorily with a jest. "Yes, I'll give them land and provide them with stone, wood and labour. I'll give them as much land as the snow falls on tomorrow morning." That was Lord Egremont's joke for the following morning would be midsummer's day. The next morning looking out from the castle towards the sea, to his amazement he saw that the land for about three miles was covered with snow. Realising that this was the work of someone more powerful than man, he immediately kept his promise and gave orders for a haven of rest to be built for St. Bega.

Rottin—The Viking

A N Egremont journalist, using the pen name "Copeland," unearthed an old pamphlet dealing with the legend of Rottington. It was originally written in verse. On a summer's day a stately Viking barque left fair Mona's Isle for the coast of

Cumbria, and its crew was composed of a bloodthirsty fierce band of raiders. Fiercest of all was the fair haired giant, Rottin, the chieftain. His swaggering gait, magnificent physique and dashing manner caused most women to fall an easy prey to this fascinating Norseman; but little cared he for women's wiles. For a while he would dally, then leave behind a trail of broken hearts. One who had madly loved him but having been spurned was now sworn to hatred, was a woman he had left behind on Mona's Isle.

As the nuns of St. Bees Abbey slept peacefully on that summer's night, their Abbess, Hilda, knelt before the altar. It was during this hour of solitude that two giant hands closed about her and she was borne away, while to her ears came the agonising cries of fear as her sisters from the convent were dragged from their beds. Hilda and her sisters were carried to Fleswick where the Vikings had made their camp. Each black robed nun was to become worse than a slave, the plaything of some lustful, cruel seaman.

Gentle Hilda, who until this hour had no evil thought for anyone in the world, conceived a deep hatred for Rottin, a hatred which smouldered even as he caressed her. One morning, some time later, while the Vikings pillaged and desecrated Cumbrian homes, Hilda looked westward over the sea. Towards her in a small boat came two occupants. Down to the shore she went, praying for a chance to escape. A lady of surpassing beauty, accompanied by her slave, stepped on to the beach. And while they stood facing each other—this scorned mistress from Mona and the Abbess—the fate of Rottin was sealed.

The plot was hatched, a packet passed from her of Mona to Hilda; then the boat with only the slave aboard passed swiftly round the headland. At the close of day, Rottin and his men returned tired and hungry. Having taken his fill of the good food prepared by the nuns, he called loudly for drink, and Hilda again and again refilled his goblet. Then with the poison beginning to have its effect, he became drowsy and stretched his huge form across the entrance of his cave.

Softly came the voice of a woman, a voice he had so often heard in Mona. Vainly the giant tried to rouse himself, but the drug administered by Hilda had done its work. The woman from Mona, snatching a bodkin from her hair, attacked him unmercifully, and so accomplished the vengeance she had sworn. The bones of the alleged St. Bees giant are said to be those of Rottin—the Viking.

Moresby Hall Legend

THERE is a legend concerning Moresby Hall, near White-haven, that today is almost forgotten. In one of the interior courts a silvery spring gushed from beneath its walls, and the source of the flow was an unsolvable secret. An old description reads: "Like similar illusory beliefs concerning buried wealth, especially such as was regarded to be deposited in sites known to have been occupied as Roman Stations, a strong belief was current among the Moresby people that there existed a great treasure hidden beneath the old hall, and that the deposit was guarded by supernatural means."

Thus from age to age the story was handed down that on a certain night a magic fountain emptied its crystal waters into the vaults, and formed a tiny lake. On its diamond-like bosom the guardian angel of the House of Moresby, in the shape of a swan, was dimly seen to float, while the faint measure of her song filled the cavernous recesses with a passionate lament for the extinction of that proud old family.

The tradition goes on to aver that should the daring wight who hears the phantom's wail be heir to that mysterious knowledge left by the Druids he will be given power to approach the fountain and drain its spell-bound waters. Then will his good fortune be amazingly increased by the vast hoards of wealth preserved under fairies' care; and if time has cast it among the ruins, and common eyes cannot discern the enchanted lake, or hear the Elfin strain, they are nevertheless there and will be so long as the Hall endures.

How long the legend has been in vogue will never be known. But strange to say, that untold wealth was deep down in the earth beneath the Moresby Hall, wealth that even to this day has not dried up. For in the bowels of the earth in this particular area is one of the richest coal mines in Great Britain.

The Wheels of Whillimoor

THE wheels of Whillimoor are difficult to explain. These three grass grown circles are situated on a moor near White-haven, and to this date still puzzle the historians. An old Furness rhyme says:

At Peel of Fouldrey we came in,
At Wheels of Whillimoor begin.

The allusion to the Peel of Fouldrey evidently refers to the landing of Martin Schwartz and his German soldiers at that place in the attempt of Lambert Simnel to dethrone Henry VII. The effort ended disastrously at the Battle of Stoke in 1497. The mention of the "Wheels of Whillimoor" in the rhyme has nothing to do with Schwartz's landing, for historians tell us that the rebels never marched in that direction.

In Cumberland, a "Whillimoor lion" was the definition given to a weak individual who was anything but a lion in spirit. One can sometimes hear the tag used today by older farming people. Whillimoor was certainly known for its cheeses, which were hard and leathery. The vendors of such cheeses attended the fairs at Rosley, Keswick, Wigton and Carlisle.

Robert Anderson, the Cumberland Bard, wrote: "At these fairs are sold a species of cheese called 'Willymer.' It is as remarkable for its poverty as Stilton is for its richness, and its surface is so hard that it frequently bids defiance to the keenest edge of a Cumbrian gully." A gully is a large bread knife. Whether the Wheels of Whillimoor are a natural symbol of Whillimoor cheese is not known.

Arlecdon Church

THERE is an old tradition that several attempts were made to build a church in what is known as Jackson's Park, Arlecdon, but as often as it was in course of construction by day, some unknown and evil hand destroyed it by night. Eventually the attempt was abandoned and the church was built in its present position.

Ghost Ship on the Solway

I HAVE met several people who have stated they have seen a ghost ship sailing along the Solway. At Allonby, an old villager said he had seen the ghost ship several times, always about Christmas time. Elliott O'Donnell, a well known writer on ghostly happenings, has mentioned the Solway ghost ship in one of his books. Trying to trace this ship, and the legend attached to it, was no easy matter. But one day by chance I turned over the pages of some old copies of the *Whitehaven News*, and came across the report of a legend which may have something to do with this weird craft.

It was night time on Christmas Eve as the ship, the *Betsy Jane*, sailed down the coast of the Solway Firth. In the nearby ports the "waits" were singing carols and the church bells were ringing. But the godless skipper of the *Betsy Jane* swore by all the powers of light and darkness that the bells might ring until they cracked, and the gleemen might roar themselves voiceless, but nevertheless it would be the chink of his gold that would chime over the self-same scenes the next Christmas morning.

Out of the Firth with his reckless crew of cut-throats headed the skipper, and steered the *Betsy Jane* to Cumbria's coast, there to trade in the profitable cargo of human beings—all to be sold into slavery. Load after Load of wretched humanity, carried under vile conditions, he shipped to the western countries, and with each shipment, fatter grew his tainted purse.

The more bodies he could ship and sell, the more bright gold there was for his greedy palms. He had one great desire—to finish by sailing up the Solway a wealthy man. At last his greedy soul was satisfied, and when the sun was low he sailed the *Betsy Jane* towards England and home, timing his return to reach the Solway on that Christmas morn, as he had so often boasted. And as the leagues rolled past him he gloated over the heavy load of bright glittering gold and rare ivory the ship carried.

But on that Christmas morn, while the carols rang out and the bells heralded a new day, the Great Power, who made all black slaves as well as white captains, took a hand in the affairs of man. With a mighty crash, the slave ship struck the fearful Giltstone Rock. The frightful groans, curses and shrieks from the floundering ship were unheard by those people ashore, who with their carolling and bell ringing were rejoicing in the coming of another Christmas Day. All the gold in the universe could not save the captain and his crew, and the waves of the Solway closed over the *Betsy Jane* and every person aboard her.

So, about Christmas time, the *Betsy Jane* sails again and again along the Solway, while the skipper tries in vain to dock his untold wealth. The years roll by, the church bells at Whitehaven, Workington, Maryport, Allonby and Silloth ring out each Christmas morn, and the *Betsy Jane* still sails on and on, never to reach port.

The Bowness Bells

THE village of Bowness on Solway is pleasantly situated on a rocky headland overlooking the Solway Firth. It is ten miles from Wigton and fourteen from Carlisle. This is the lowest point of the estuary which is fordable at low water. It was formerly used as a short cut to Scotland and was often crossed by the border raiders.

Tradition tells us that a battle was once fought on the sands between the English and the Scots and as the waters rose the combatants carried on the melee further inland. Whether it was on the English side or the Scottish side is not recorded, but both sides claim it was on the other's soil. The legend attached to St. Michael's church concerns its bells. It appears that the Scot raiders, crossing the sands for the purpose of pilfering, hit on the idea of stealing the church bells from Bow-

ness, so that no future alarm could be given when they made further visits. Everything went according to plan until the Scots began to make their crossing when unfortunately for them the tide came in earlier than had been expected and so they and their loot, including the bells, sank deep down into the tide-covered sands.

The Bowness men swore revenge. One can read much about the Scots raiding England and stealing wives and cattle, but little is recorded in Cumberland history of raids made by Cumbrians on the border Scottish towns and villages. St. Michael's church, however, is existing proof that such raids took place. Not only did the Bowness men bring back the bonnie Scottish lassies and cattle, but as revenge for the previous raid they also took the bells from an Annan church which they had so often heard faintly ringing in the distance, and had them installed in the belfry of St. Michael's church.

Many attempts were made by the outraged Scots to regain their lost bells and restore them to their rightful place, but without success. Even to this day, when a new vicar is inducted at St. Michael's church, Bowness on Solway, the Annan Provost sends a request for the return of the stolen property.

8. The Cumberland Plain

Mackerin Tarn

MACKERIN TARN, near Cockermouth, has a Welsh legend attached to it. It is said that Mackerin was the site of the city and castle of Morken, King of Cumbria. Jocelyn of Furness states that this king was buried there in the royal town of "Thropmorken". The people of this royal town displeased the Almighty who sent terrific storms and earthquakes to destroy the people and all their buildings.

Great Broughton

THE village of Great Broughton in West Cumberland is part of the 2,063 acre parish of Broughton. The manor of Broughton, including Broughton Moor, was given by Waltheof, Lord of Allerdale, with his sister in marriage to Waltheof, son of Gilmin, whose posterity adopted the name of Broughton, and resided here for several generations. The line appears to have become extinct about the reign of Henry VI (1422-1461), and the manor reverted to the Earls of Northumberland as Lords of Allerdale.

Above the banks of the Derwent at Great Broughton there was once the Chapel of St. Lawrence, and its site was visible to all, because no matter what crop was grown in the large field which contained the outline of the graveyard, the churchyard itself was never ploughed.

The legend says that, try as they might, the farm-hands could not plough that holy piece of ground. Horses harnessed to the ploughs would rear in fright, and dig their hooves firmly into the ground when there was a sign of the plough touching the sacred spot. It is only since the introduction of the tractor that this place has been ploughed, and a local farmer says that even the tractor gives them trouble in the sacred area.

The Lion that Ran Away

PAPCASTLE, formerly a town in Bridekirk, is associated
with an eccentric character who was born there in the early
part of last century. In the first part of his life he was a much
admired and respected writing master, but his extraordinary
turn for wit and humour led him into improper company.
Later he spent some time painting signs for inns, in which he
spent most of his time drinking.

Being once employed to paint a lion by an innkeeper, he
requested to be allowed to paint it chained, but the innkeeper
would not agree. Salathiel Court, for that was the artist's name,
decided to get even with the innkeeper, and so he painted a
beautiful sign in water colours. It was greatly admired for
several days, but as soon as the rain came it vanished.

This caused endless amusement among the Papcastle
inhabitants, but the innkeeper was wild with rage and accused
Salathiel of unfair dealing, to which he replied: "You refused,
Master, to let me paint a chain on your lion, so can I help it
if it has run away?" He afterwards painted a sign in oils
which remained for many years. Court eventually became
bellman at Whitehaven, where he once cried a lost purse:

A big fat Frenchman lost his purse,
And he can't find it, which is worse;
He that lost it, let him seek it,
He that found it, let him keep it.

Sebergham Church and William Wastell

A PRETTY little hamlet situated near Wigton is called
Sebergham. It lies in the Caldew Vale and was the birthplace
of the Cumberland bard, Josiah Relph. He spent his leisure
hours on Crag Top, and had a chair and table hewn out of
solid rock. The legend of Sebergham Church is interesting and
romantic. In the year 1188 there lived in this beautiful part of
Cumberland a hermit named William Wastell, who made
himself a clearing in the forest that existed there, and he
gathered together sufficient people to form a colony. This
was the origin of this hamlet of Sebergham.

There are scanty records of Wastell's mode of living, but it
can only be surmised that his cave or cell was selected here
because he wished to find some remote corner where he could
be assured of peaceful retirement. It is possible that he was a
fugitive from some kind of enemy. Apparently Wastell was

not without spiritual leanings for he erected a small chapel for his community.

It was either King John or Henry III who secured to him by charter the land which he had cleared. At his death he left this land to the Priory of Carlisle, on condition that the Prior accepted the responsibility for the spiritual welfare of the people. The Prior's Church was built over Wastell's Chapel and, during the course of repairs in 1775, four fine lancet windows were discovered beneath a layer of concrete and plaster. The ill-proportioned tower was erected in 1825 in the face of much opposition from the parishioners. The following protest notice was pinned to the door of the church on the day the tower was completed:

> *The Priest and the miller built the church steeple*
> *Without the consent or goodwill of the people,*
> *A tax to collect they tried to impose,*
> *In defiance of right and subversion of laws,*
> *The matter remains in a state of suspension*
> *And likely to be the sad bone of contention.*
> *If concession be made to agree with us all,*
> *Let the tax be applied to build the church wall.*
> *Church wall now in a ruinous state.*

—Sebergham Bound, Juiy 12th 1826

Radiant Boy

IN a superstitious area, one is sure to find ghostly traditions attached to the county families, and the Lake District is no exception. One of the most popular of such legends is attributed to Corby Castle and its "Radiant Boy". This has been described as a luminous apparition which makes its appearance with dire results.

The tradition was that the member of the family who saw the Radiant Boy would rise to great power and then afterwards die a violent death. The only proof of this legend, so far as is known, was that of Lord Castlereagh who committed suicide in 1822.

Corby Castle, on the pretty banks of the fast rushing Eden, a few miles from Carlisle, housed the Howards of Corby for several centuries, all of whom attained eminence in various walks of life, as warriors, as statesmen, as writers and as philosophers. None, however, seem to have come to an untimely death, nor for that matter is it recorded that any of them ever saw the "Radiant Boy."

Talkin Tarn

TALKIN Tarn is a small but lovely lake covering sixty acres. It is situated only a short distance from Brampton, an old English town where Bonnie Prince Charlie was pleased to make his headquarters while he awaited an onslaught by the Royal forces from Newcastle. Talkin Tarn is about seven miles from Carlisle, and is not as well known as it might be. The natives of the village of Talkin still believe the tarn to be bottomless. The legend according to an old poem tells how the original village of Brampton was destroyed by an earthquake.

One day an old man walked into Brampton in a distressed and tired state. He had come far and was sure he would receive food and rest from the hospitable Cumbrians. But the people of Brampton at that time were known to be of a both cruel and selfish nature. They ignored the old man's pleas for food and shelter and turned their dogs on him.

The old vagrant staggered to the centre of the village and dropped down on his knees and appealed to the Almighty to punish the people of Brampton for their selfishness. Then he staggered on towards the city of Carlisle. Within a short time his prayer was answered, for the heavens opened with torrents of rain, a tremendous earthquake took place and houses disappeared into the bowels of the earth. And in the morning, where the village of Brampton stood, was a still, deep and mysterious lake. I have heard it said that by taking a boat into the centre of the tarn one can look down and see ruins of old buildings, which rather contradicts the idea that the Tarn is bottomless. Peter Burn, a Brampton poet of the last century, described the tragic end of the original village in his poem:

> *God in the stillness of the night,*
> *So I've heard old people say,*
> *An earthquake sent unto this place*
> *And moved the whole away.*
> *Where stood the village spoken of,*
> *Now a glassy lake is seen,*
> *No sign is left to indicate*
> *That their houses once had been.*
> *Ye Cumbrians! Oft repeat it,*
> *Let your sons this legend know;*
> *They may learn anon the lesson—*
> *Sin does not unpunished go.*

There is a similar legend connected with Urswick Lake or Tarn, in the Furness district. An old poem tells the story, a few lines of which are as follows:

> *The peasants tell that years ago*
> *In the time of the vengeful Dane,*
> *That a village stood where the watery flood*
> *Now covers o'er the plain.*
> *But the earthquake's might*
> *In the dark midnight*
> *Had sunk that village so far from sight*
> *In a deep and watery grave.*

No doubt the people in these small villages believed that the earthquakes were the vengeance of God for some wrong-doing.

Lizzie o' Branton

A WITCH who was well known over a very wide area was Lizzie Batty, or as she was more often called, Lizzie o' Branton. She lived in a little cottage on the pretty roadside between Brampton and Talkin Tarn. She acted in a peculiar manner as becomes any witch; she spoke to the birds of the air and beasts of the field, and kept lamed birds and deformed

animals about her abode. She dressed curiously, with the consequence that she was credited with many supernatural powers.

Lizzie told people she could control the elements, and if
rain was badly needed by the farmers only she could make it
rain. It needed the bribe of a sack of potatoes or a chunk
of bacon or ham before she would oblige the farmers with the
weather they wanted.

She died in the year 1817 at the age of eighty-eight. The
day of her funeral was long remembered in Brampton as the
stormiest day the town had ever seen. In fact, many natives
thought that this second Brampton was about to suffer the
fate of the first Brampton and be consigned to the bottom of
Talkin Tarn. Although it was March, darkness came just
after noon, so suddenly the lanterns were lighted at the
grave side, only to be extinguished again and again by the fury
of the tempest.

A tradition still lingers that those who bore the coffin to the
grave solemnly affirmed it was empty and the body gone.
Until recently it was common in the district for a mother
to warn her children "that Lizzie o' Branton u'll git yer if ye
divvent behave."

THERE are many more legends still in existence, although
one finds a certain similarity between the legend of one
district and that of another. One can only conclude by saying
that the Lakelanders are born story-tellers. There is nothing
they like better than having a real good Cumbrian "crack."

I believe that in the lonely districts, when living in the

valleys beneath the towering high mountains, one can let the
imagination run riot and picture all kinds of shapes and
happenings. The "Lion and the Lamb" for example, high up
on the mountain alongside Dunmail Raise, a huge stone
image made by nature, needs no flight of imagination. Can
one wonder then that, in the days before most people could
read or write in this district, they wove their own stories about
what they saw, and then passed them on from one generation
to another?